SandCastle™
Unusual Pets

Portly Potbellied Pigs

Alex Kuskowski
AUTHOR

C.A. Nobens
ILLUSTRATOR

Consulting Editor, Diane Craig, M.A./Reading Specialist

A Division of ABDO

ABDO
Publishing Company

visit us at www.abdopublishing.com

Published by ABDO Publishing Company, a division of ABDO, P.O. Box 398166, Minneapolis, Minnesota 55439. Copyright © 2013 by Abdo Consulting Group, Inc. International copyrights reserved in all countries. No part of this book may be reproduced in any form without written permission from the publisher. SandCastle™ is a trademark and logo of ABDO Publishing Company.

Printed in the United States of America, North Mankato, Minnesota
102012
012013

 PRINTED ON RECYCLED PAPER

Editor: Liz Salzmann
Content Developer: Nancy Tuminelly
Cover and Interior Design and Production: Kelly Doudna, Mighty Media, Inc.
Photo Credits: Ross Heywood, iStockPhoto (picturistic), Shutterstock

Library of Congress Cataloging-in-Publication Data

Kuskowski, Alex.
  Portly potbellied pigs / by Alex Kuskowski ; illustrator C.A. Nobens.
     p. cm. -- (Unusual pets)
  ISBN 978-1-61783-401-1
  1. Potbellied pigs as pets--Juvenile literature. I. Nobens, C. A., ill. II. Title.
  SF393.P74K87 2013
  636.4'0887--dc23
                              2011050812

SandCastle™ Level: Transitional

SandCastle™ books are created by a team of professional educators, reading specialists, and content developers around five essential components—phonemic awareness, phonics, vocabulary, text comprehension, and fluency—to assist young readers as they develop reading skills and strategies and increase their general knowledge. All books are written, reviewed, and leveled for guided reading, early reading intervention, and Accelerated Reader® programs for use in shared, guided, and independent reading and writing activities to support a balanced approach to literacy instruction. The SandCastle™ series has four levels that correspond to early literacy development. The levels are provided to help teachers and parents select appropriate books for young readers.

Emerging Readers
(no flags)

Beginning Readers
(1 flag)

Transitional Readers
(2 flags)

Fluent Readers
(3 flags)

Contents

Unusual Pets

Unusual pets can be interesting and fun! Unusual pets might also eat unusual food. They might have special care needs. It is a good idea to learn about your new friend before bringing it home.

There are special laws for many unusual animals. Make sure the kind of pet you want is allowed in your city and state.

Potbellied Pig Basics

Type of animal
Potbellied pigs are **mammals**.

Adult size
60 to 200 pounds (27 to 90 kg)

Life expectancy
10 to 15 years

Natural habitat
fields of
Southeastern
Asia

Potbellied pigs eat vegetables, meat, and fruit. Today, Josie feeds her pig apples.

Potbellied pigs need to spend time outside. Amber's piglet plays in the fresh grass.

Potbellied pigs love attention. Danielle plays with her pig after school.

Potbellied pigs have very good noses. They use them to **sniff** out treats.

A Potbellied Pig Story

My **cousin** lives in Idaho
and his name is Ziggy.
He's very proud of his pet,
a pig that he named Piggy!

Piggy is a clever **swine**.
She can do most anything.
She can dance and she can add.
She jumps right through a ring!

They have entered a talent show.

It is happening next week.

Ziggy is teaching Piggy

to kiss him on the cheek!

Every day they practice.

They really want to win.

The **trophy** is the largest

that it has ever been.

Ziggy is surprised
on the day of the big show.
In walks Stephanie Smith
with a skating crocodile in tow!

Ziggy waits for his turn.
He sees the croc skate past.
Those two are really great.
Can he and Piggy last?

Finally it's Piggy's turn.

People clap and cheer out loud.

Piggy runs around and dances.

She even paints some clouds!

The **competition** is very close.

The judges can't decide.

Then they say that Piggy won!

Ziggy beams with pride!

Fun Facts

* Pigs have no body odor.

* Most pigs have stiff hairs along their backs. They stick up when the pigs are happy or upset.

* People have been raising pigs for more than 10,000 years.

* Potbellied pigs were first brought to North America in the 1980s.

Potbellied Pig Quiz

Read each sentence below. Then decide whether it is true or false!

1. Pigs don't eat vegetables.

2. Potbellied pigs should never go outside.

3. Potbellied pigs love attention.

4. Piggy is a clever **swine**.

5. Ziggy and Piggy got second place at the talent show.

Answers: 1. False 2. False 3. True 4. True 5. False

Glossary

awe – a feeling of wonder and respect.

competition – a contest.

cousin – the child of your aunt or uncle.

mammal – a warm-blooded animal that has hair and whose females produce milk to feed their young.

sniff – to smell something.

swine – a hog or pig.

trophy – a prize given to the winner of a competition.

The Oregon Trail™

The text was set in Garamond.
The display text was set in Pixel-Western, Press Start 2P, and Slim Thin Pixelettes.
Illustrations by Jani Orban, June Brigman, Yancey Labat, Ron Wagner, Hi-Fi Color
Design, and Walden Font Co.

ISBN: 978-1-328-55003-3 paper over board
ISBN: 978-1-328-54999-0 paperback

Printed in the United States of America
DOC 10 9 8 7 6 5 4 3 2 1
4500722661

The Oregon Trail

4

THE ROAD TO OREGON CITY

by JESSE WILEY

Houghton Mifflin Harcourt
BOSTON   NEW YORK

1850
Oregon City
OREGON
TERRITORY
Three Island Crossing
CALIFORNIA
UTAH
TERRITORY
NEW MEXIC
TERRITORY
Legend
Oregon Trail
TERRITORIES
State Lines
(Modern Day)

OREGON TRAIL

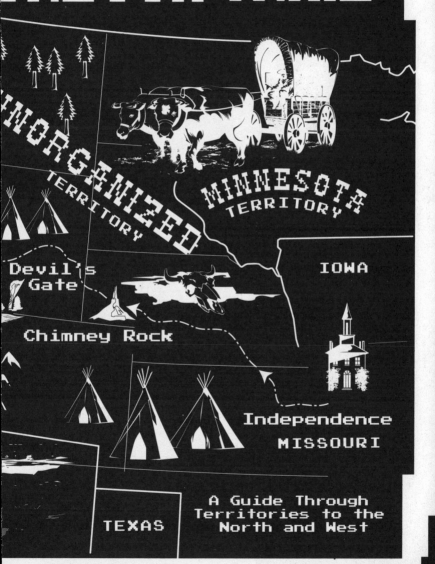

UNORGANIZED TERRITORY

MINNESOTA TERRITORY

Devil's Gate

IOWA

Chimney Rock

Independence

MISSOURI

TEXAS

A Guide Through Territories to the North and West

The Oregon Trail

GO WEST
Complete the Journey

You are a young settler headed out West by wagon train in the year 1850. You and your family are on the last leg of the dangerous frontier journey known as the Oregon Trail. You have crossed more than 1,300 miles of territory in what will later become the states of Kansas, Nebraska, Wyoming, and Idaho.

For fifteen miles a day for more than three months, you have walked beside your oxen and covered wagon with your family. You can't ride in the wagon because it holds everything you need for the journey and for your family's new lives as farmers in Oregon.

You've crossed mountains, deserts, and prairies, and you've passed through Devil's Gate and the perilous Snake River. You've also faced wild animals, dealt with raging forest fires, and learned how to survive in deadly desert conditions by traveling at night. You now know how to handle livestock and trade what you have. Best of all, there's still adventure ahead of you—*if* you can survive the steep and treacherous trek through areas like the hot, sandy Bruneau Dunes; the Cascade Rapids; the surging Columbia River; the bubbling Soda Springs; Fort Boise; Flagstaff Hill, which signals the start of the Blue Mountains; the Barlow Toll Road; and after that, the steep descent of Laurel Hill, near Mount Hood.

You've met indigenous people of various Nations like the Arapaho, Lakota, Shoshone, and Osage.

Only one path will lead you safely through this book to your destination, Oregon City, but there are twenty-three other possible endings, full of risks and surprises. Along the way, no matter what path you choose, you will experience natural disasters, sickness, and other hazards of the Trail.

You're trapped underneath the ice! How will you survive?

A deadly lynx is about to pounce!

Bandits are lurking nearby; what will you do?

Before you begin, make sure to read the Guide to the Trail at the back of the book, starting on page 170. It's filled with important information you'll need to make wise choices.

You're not alone, and you can make decisions with friends, people you meet along the way, or Ma and Pa—but also trust your good judgment. Use the resources you have, and you'll find your way to the end of the Trail at Oregon City, where you'll get your own plot of land to build a farmhouse and start a new life with your family!

Every second counts!
Think fast.
What will you do?

➔ Ready? ⬅

BLAZE A TRAIL TO

OREGON CITY!

Three Island Crossing

AUGUST 31, 1850

You dip your hands into the warm water and splash it over your hot, sweaty face. It's so refreshing to wash the grime off your skin after being on the dusty trail that you can't help but smile.

The water is lapping at you like a soft, wet tongue . . . until suddenly you wake up, reach out, and feel something furry.

"Archie! Yuck!" you groan, pushing your dog away from where he's been licking your face.

Archie just looks at you with his big brown eyes and wags his tail.

"It's all right, boy." You laugh, scratching him around the ears as the five-a.m. bugle sounds. It's barely light outside your tent, but it's time to start the morning chores, eat breakfast, pack up your wagon, and get back on the Trail.

It's already been almost four months since you started your journey from Independence, Missouri, back in May. But every morning, it's a little harder to get up.

"Wake up, Samuel." You nudge your little brother, fast asleep beside you. "You need to milk Daisy."

"You do it," Samuel moans, rolling over on his feather mat.

Hannah, your little sister, marches into your tent. She's always been the earliest riser among you. Samuel used to be more energized in the morning, but as you've made your way through the difficult Rocky Mountains, he's needed more rest. Plus, instead of traveling fifteen miles a day, your wagon train has been covering only about ten to twelve miles because of the rugged and treacherous terrain.

"Ma says to hurry up," Hannah says, her bonnet sliding halfway over her eyes as usual. "She needs you to get fuel for the fire, and Sam to milk—"

"Daisy," Samuel mutters, cutting her off. "I know, I know. I'm coming."

Hannah rolls her eyes at him and goes back to help Ma prepare breakfast. You don't blame Samuel for being grumpy as he packs up his bed and carries it out of the tent. Your body longs for more rest too. But you know you don't have that option. The wagon train will roll out in about an hour and a half, and you need to help Ma and Pa get everything ready.

Your stomach growls as you anticipate breakfast, which will probably be flapjacks and bacon . . . again. Since you've left Independence with a wagon led by a team of oxen piled high with everything you own, you've eaten more bacon than you ever dreamed was possible. Ma has been pretty creative with the few other foods you've carried with you for more than 1,400 miles so far: flour, cornmeal, sugar, coffee, salt, and beans. But it's still gotten boring. Luckily, you've also eaten whatever you have been able to catch along the Trail, including rabbits, squirrels, deer, and buffalo, along with fruits and berries.

"I can't wait to get to Oregon City and eat at a tavern again," Hannah says as if she is reading your mind.

"Me too, Hannah," you say. "If there even *are* any taverns."

Your family is traveling out West to claim the land available to anyone willing to make the trip. Other emigrants like you have already made it to Oregon City and started their lives. But you don't really know what to expect when you get there.

You've covered two-thirds of your trek, through prairie, desert, and now mountains. The sights along the way have been incredible, from steep cliffs to massive waterfalls to enormous rock formations, and more. And you've overcome a number of challenges, including dangerous river crossings, ferocious animals, and serious illnesses.

"Good morning," Caleb says as you walk past him with an armful of brush for the campfire. Caleb has proved to be an excellent wagon captain over the journey. His son and daughter, Joseph and Eliza, have become the best friends you've ever had.

"Good morning," you reply. "What's ahead on the Trail today?"

"We are going to have a meeting after we all fuel

up on breakfast," Caleb replies. "There's a big decision to make."

You feel a familiar tinge of excitement, wondering what the decision will be as you hurry back to your campsite and help Ma start a big fire. As the bacon starts sizzling in the iron skillet, you grind coffee beans and make a strong brew that everyone, even Hannah, drinks. You've all grown accustomed to drinking coffee on the Trail and are grateful it masks some of the bad-tasting water you are forced to use along the way.

Pa fixes you a plate of flapjacks, and you sink your teeth into a thick, buttery pancake. You wish there was some syrup but are grateful for your cow Daisy's steady supply of cream that Ma churns into butter by hanging a bucket on the side of the wagon as it bumps along the rocky terrain.

"Pa, do you know what big decision we have to make today?" you say.

"Yes. We need to choose whether or not to cross the Snake River two more times and head toward Fort Boise," Pa starts.

"That river again!" Hannah interrupts.

You shiver, remembering the ordeal you just went through at Three Island Crossing. You had never been more terrified than when Ma fell into the water, but luckily Pa was quick to save her.

"What's the other choice?" Samuel asks.

"We would take the South Alternate Route," Pa explains. "It goes south of the Snake River but runs along it, so you don't have to cross."

"Isn't that better, then?" Ma asks.

"I don't know," Pa answers. "It would take us through the Bruneau Sand Dunes. They are hot, dry, and dusty."

Your family sits quietly and ponders the options.

"I'm afraid to cross the river again," Ma says.

"Me too," adds Hannah.

"I'm worried about the dry conditions of the alternate route," Pa says. "It might be hard on the animals."

"And I hate being thirsty," Samuel adds, agreeing with Pa.

Everyone looks at you.

"It looks like you have to be the one to help us decide what we tell Caleb," Pa says. "What do you think we should do?"

You consider everything carefully. Even though the river crossings are dangerous, at least you know

what to expect. You're not sure what the dunes will be like. On the other hand, the idea of two more crossings is daunting.

What do you say?

If you pick the regular route, turn to page 138

If you pick the alternate route, turn to page 108

You sit in front of the fire and frantically rub your feet. Ma returns with the dishes.

"My goodness! How did this happen?" Ma says with a gasp when she spots your purple toes. You hold up a shoe and show her a worn sole. She takes it and walks over to Pa. You try wiggling your toes, but they are not moving as Pa rushes over to you.

"Does it hurt?" Pa asks.

"I can't really feel anything," you reply.

Pa nods at you and tries to smile, but he seems worried. He walks away to find the vet, the member of your wagon train with the most medical knowledge of the group. Ma sits with you and rubs your feet for a bit. After a few minutes, Pa returns with the vet, who presses firmly on your toes.

"Can you feel that?" the vet asks you.

"No," you respond, feeling scared.

The vet tells Pa to wrap your feet in a blanket and have you sit in front of the fire for the night. Ma bundles your feet tightly and you finally fall asleep, hoping that your feet will be back to normal by morning.

The bugle sounds, and you rush to unwrap your feet.

"Ma!" you shout, pointing to your feet, which are black all the way up to your ankles. Ma runs to get the vet, and soon a crowd is standing around you.

"This is terrible," the vet says. "But your feet can't be saved. If we don't remove them, you will lose your legs."

You start screaming before he finishes speaking.

Your family uses the rest of their money on supplies to help you heal after your surgery.

Oregon City is no longer in your future.

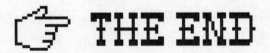 **THE END**

You decide to give your parents time to recover before making them continue on the journey. Even if they were to rest in the wagon, there wouldn't be room for both of them to lie down. Plus, you know how bumpy and uncomfortable the ride would be. And the truth is, the idea of leading your wagon alone without Pa makes you nervous.

Hannah and Samuel help you do all the chores that Ma and Pa usually do. You fix meals, but Pa is still having trouble eating anything. It frightens you

to see his face so drawn and pale. Luckily, Ma seems to be improving slightly.

"I think your soup is making me stronger," she says with a weak smile.

Then, the next morning, Pa doesn't wake up. You hear Ma shouting and run over to where he is. You lean over to check whether he is breathing, but you can't hear anything.

"Pa!" you shout, shaking him. "Wake up, Pa!"

He remains motionless. You throw some water on his face to try to wake him up, but nothing happens.

"What do we do?" you finally cry, clinging to Ma.

Ma is barely strong enough to stand, but she tries everything to wake Pa. However, Pa doesn't open his eyes again. As night falls, you hear Ma sobbing in her tent and you realize that life as you know it has changed. Your body starts shaking as fear and grief fill your heart. How can you go on without Pa? Then it hits you. With Pa gone, you are in charge. Ma, Hannah, and Samuel are too beside themselves to make any decisions. You wish you could wake up and find that this is all a terrible nightmare. But it isn't. Your family is going to look to you now, so you try to think clearly and decide what to do. Do you head back to Fort Boise and try to find your way back to Kentucky, where you have family? Or do you push onward to Oregon and honor Pa's dream?

If you head back to Fort Boise, turn to page **145**

If you continue to Oregon, turn to page **53**

I think we should camp," you say. "It'll be hard to keep walking and carry our things."

"And I'm too hungry," Hannah adds, while Samuel nods.

"Okay," Ma agrees, looking at all of you with concern. "I just hope we catch something soon."

Pa goes out to set the traps and try to hunt. But he comes back a few hours later with only one small bird.

"This is all I could catch, and I wasted a lot of bullets trying to catch things that weren't a good shot." He hangs his head.

Ma roasts the bird, and you each get a small piece. You savor every morsel and lick your fingers, still hungry. Poor Archie is left with the bones. His ribs are sticking out, and as you look at him, you wonder how skinny you must have gotten too.

The next morning, you hear hooves approaching. Pa draws his rifle, tensed. But it's fur trappers, who scour the area.

"It looks like you've fallen on hard times," one of the men says as he dismounts his horse.

"Yes, sir," Pa says. "I'm afraid we could use your help."

"I can help you hunt, and give you a bit of this dried buffalo jerky," the man offers.

Ma accepts the jerky gratefully and parcels it out to each of you. You try not to gobble it up and instead chew it slowly to make it last. Then Ma fixes coffee, and you each sip a nice hot cup. When you're done, your stomach doesn't feel as empty. But a few hours later, your stomach is rumbling again, and this time not because you're hungry. You end up getting severe cramps and diarrhea. Next comes vomiting and fever, and then the worst of all. You die of dysentery.

 **THE END**

I think it might make the most sense to leave the wagon," you say, surprising yourself. The path has been so difficult and you're so close to Oregon City that you just want to get there as quickly as you can.

The rest of your family agrees and sorts through the things you will load onto the oxen. You take only your valuables, food, clothes, bedrolls, and essential cooking and camping supplies.

"I can't believe we're just leaving the wagon," Hannah says sadly.

"And all these things," Samuel adds, peering into it.

"Well, I have to say, I feel a bit lighter now," Pa says, trying to be cheerful. "And we should move much faster."

As Pa predicted, you are able to cover much more ground over the next few days. But soon you realize that your food supply is not going to get you to Oregon City.

"A few men are volunteering to scout for food while the rest remain camped," Caleb says to Pa. "What do you think?"

"Don't you think we should all stick together?" Ma asks, looking worried.

"I won't go if you don't want me to," Pa says, looking at all of you.

You exchange looks with Ma. Without saying a word, you know she feels the same as you. She doesn't want Pa to leave you behind, but at the same time she realizes the reasons he needs to go.

What do you say?

If you ask Pa not to go, turn to page 60

If you tell Pa it's okay for him to go, turn to page 74

Everyone wants to get out of the desert-like conditions as quickly as possible and votes for going through the dunes.

"Okay, so it looks like we have a hike ahead of us tomorrow," Caleb says. "Rest up, everybody."

"I'm too hot to rest," Samuel complains. "And I'm always thirsty."

You feel a rush of sympathy for your little brother, whose temperature is always running hotter than the rest of your family's. And you also have a small pang of guilt. He wasn't keen on coming this way all along and has been finding it difficult.

"I have a piece of honey candy," Joseph offers Samuel. "Will that help?"

Samuel takes the candy gratefully and sucks on it in silence as you help to prepare camp.

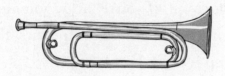

The next morning when the early bugle sounds, everyone gets ready for the day's hike through the dunes. If all goes well, you should be well across them by your midday break.

Everything goes smoothly for a while. The animals pull the wagons without a hitch, and Pa smiles, pleased with the progress. But when you reach halfway up the dunes, your wagon is stuck! The oxen keep pulling the wagon and straining, but it won't budge. And when Pa tries to help push it out, it just sinks deeper into the sand.

Finally, with a tremendous amount of effort,

the wagon is freed. But in the process, your animals are overworked, and they don't recover. Soon, their carcasses line the Trail, and you are left stranded. It's too hard to go on without them, and you can't carry everything you need for the journey on your backs. Pa decides to stop at the next trading post and try to get some more oxen. If you're lucky, you might find some go-backers willing to sell you theirs. But until then, your trip is on hold.

 **THE END**

I agree," Pa says. "Let's use the rope to set traps."

You spend the rest of the afternoon making traps with Pa and are proud when you put together four strong ones. Pa asks you to come with him to set them, and you bait each with a small piece of bacon.

As night falls, Pa says it's time to check on the traps. You turn over the first three traps and find nothing. As you approach the fourth trap, you hear something struggling inside and smile at Pa.

"Sounds like a good dinner," he says. You hear a rustling and wonder if there's another small animal nearby. But it's a mountain lion! You scream and try to run, but you don't get very far.

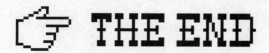 **THE END**

Everyone agrees to push through the snowstorm, since the idea of sitting around in the freezing cold and wind and waiting for it to pass seems more dangerous. Instead, you all bundle up in extra layers of clothes to keep warm, and drape all the extra blankets over the oxen. Pa feeds the animals handfuls of grain to help calm them down and give them energy to keep moving.

You trudge through the snow, amazed by how quickly everything around you is covered in a sheet of white. The cold wind is chapping any part of your skin that is exposed. Even though your scarf is wrapped around your head and much of your face, the part of your nose peeking through is freezing.

"This must be what it feels like to be a snowman," Hannah says, hugging herself for warmth as she struggles to keep up with you.

"I know," you say, imagining that your nose is as bright as a carrot.

"I wish we could play in the snow instead of having to walk all day," she says, looking wistful.

"Yeah, it's no fun to have snow if we can't even play in it," Samuel adds.

"Maybe we can play for a little while when we make camp," you say.

"If I'm not completely frozen by then," Hannah complains.

"It'll be even better if you are," you say, picking up a handful of snow and tossing it at her gently. "Snowmen are supposed to be cold, right?"

Hannah sticks out her tongue playfully and runs back to the wagon for a rest, huddling inside it with Archie for warmth.

As you hike for the next couple of hours, the wind and snow ease up and then taper off completely. By the time you stop to make camp, the sun is shining again. You help Pa set up the tents, and Ma builds a roaring fire. The animals are fed and left to recover, and then you finally have time to play until supper.

"Let's have a snowball fight," Joseph says. "We'll pick teams."

"Yeah!" Samuel says. "I want to play."

Joseph and you are the team leaders. You form your teams and then split up to plan. You pick Samuel and Eliza.

"Let's make a hundred snowballs and have them ready to use," Samuel says.

"And then let's go around that way, and plan a sneak attack on the other team," you say, pointing in the direction away from camp.

You see Joseph hiding behind a tree and decide to get him first. Samuel gives you the signal that the coast is clear. Crouching down so you can't be seen, you run around in a wide circle so he won't see you coming. You're holding two of the biggest snowballs you've ever made. As you're running, your footsteps sink into the freshly fallen snow, leaving big footprints. But then you suddenly step into a frozen pond without realizing it. With a crunch, the thin layer of ice gives way and . . .

SPLASH!

You plunge into the icy water!

Instinctively, you gasp as you fall and take in a huge breath of air before your head goes underwater.

But now you are trapped underneath the ice and have only a few minutes to act before you will run out of air.

Don't panic, you tell yourself. You look up and attempt to find the hole in the ice where you fell in. That way, you can try to climb out of it again. Underwater, the ice all looks the same to you, until you notice a darker spot to your left and a lighter spot to your right.

Which one do you slowly move toward so you can try to pull yourself out of the water?

If you move toward the darker spot, turn to page **136**

If you move toward the lighter spot, turn to page **153**

Seeing Samuel looking so cozy curled up with Archie only reminds you of how freezing you are. With that one small ember still glowing in the campfire, you grab a couple of nearby twigs and gently place them into the pit. You can put out the fire after you've warmed yourself up just a bit. You know that starting a fire when everyone else is asleep could be incredibly dangerous, but right now, you're too cold to think of anything but warming up. You blow on the embers softly to ignite the flames, but nothing happens for several minutes.

Finally, your work pays off when you see the embers glowing a warm yellow-white. Soon enough, small flames tickle the branches. You hurry to grab more kindling before the twigs die out completely, because you haven't even had a chance to really warm yourself up.

After you pile on branch after branch, watching the flames lick around the burning wood, you finally have a roaring fire that crackles and glows in the dark. You hold your trembling hands near the edge of the campfire, enjoying the way the heat travels through your fingertips to the rest of your chilled body.

But you're so exhausted, and you desperately want to lie down. Sitting on the cold, hard ground isn't entirely pleasant, even with the fire. You grab your mat and drag it over to the campfire, placing it alongside the pit to receive the greatest amount of warmth. Once you lie down, you enjoy the heat radiating off the flames. Before you know it, you burrow down into your mat and drift off to sleep.

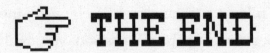

You're jolted awake by the smell of smoke and the stench of something burning. You have fallen asleep too close to the fire, and no one is awake to help you.

☞ **THE END**

We'll make camp and wait out the storm," Pa says, glancing at the clouds with a worried expression. "I just hope it passes quickly."

You help him set up the tents, struggling to get them to stand up. It's too windy to start a fire, so you eat a cold supper of prairie biscuits and jerky. And then you ask Ma if you can play in the snow.

"Okay," she says. "But not for too long. It'll be dark soon."

You, Hannah, and Samuel build a giant snow fort and hide behind it, piling up an arsenal of snowballs. Joseph and Eliza do the same on the other side of camp.

"Charge!" Joseph shouts, and the battle begins. Snowballs fill the air as you pelt one another. The cold snow stings your skin, and you finally call a truce when both sides are out of snowballs. You run in the snow and fall over, laughing.

"Let's make snow angels!" Hannah says, lying down next to you and waving her arms and legs in the snow.

"Come on back now," Ma calls.

You go back to the tents and only realize how cold it is once you've stopped running around. Even though you try to warm up under the blankets, as it gets darker, the temperature drops and you are really cold.

"I'm freezing," Samuel whines. "I can't sleep."

"Me either," Hannah adds.

Ma looks concerned.

"I was going to put these blankets on the oxen, but you better use them," she says.

Finally, huddled together, you are able to get to sleep.

By morning, the snow has stopped falling. You step out of the tent, and the thick blanket of snow reaches above your knees as you walk. After only a few moments, you hear shouting.

"The oxen!"

It's Pa! You rush over to where he is and find him looking distraught.

"Half of them have perished," he says, sounding devastated. "What will we do?"

The remaining oxen won't be able to pull the weight of the wagon on their own. Other wagons have lost animals too.

"We should have kept moving through the storm," Caleb says, sounding regretful. "We'll just have to take what we can carry on the animals. There's no other choice."

Even though you are filled with sadness over the lost animals, there's no time to waste. You spend the next few hours helping your parents sort through your things, choosing only the most important items to take with you.

While Ma and Pa are trying to attach bags to the remaining oxen and onto Daisy, Samuel runs over to you.

"Hannah and I found some wild berries," he says. "Come see!"

You follow Samuel and run over to some bushes in the distance. As you approach, you see Hannah pulling berries off the bush and filling up her apron. She looks up at you and smiles.

"Look how many I have," she says. "I hope they are good to eat."

Just then you spot something moving behind the bush. It's a bear!

You freeze, terrified. It feels like everything is happening more slowly than it really is

as the bear comes toward Hannah. You're afraid that it wants the berries and will attack her, and you have only a moment to react. Do you pick up Hannah's doll from where it is lying on the ground near you and throw it at the bear to distract it? Or do you yell for Hannah to run?

If you throw the doll, turn to page **71**

If you yell, turn to page **151**

The taste of fresh honey is too mouthwatering to resist. You relent and agree to let Joseph smoke out the bees. Joseph finds a large, heavy stick and sets it on fire, then douses the flames with his foot, creating a smoking log. He holds it up to you.

"Here, take this while I climb," he orders.

You hesitate. The bees are already swarming around you. Still, you take the smoking stick. Joseph jumps to clamber up the tree, his movements shaking the nest even more than yours first did. A bee whizzes by your ear.

"Joseph, I don't think this is a good idea," you say nervously.

"I'm almost there," he grunts. "Do you want honey or not?"

"Joseph," says Eliza, "I think we should just get down."

But Joseph ignores her and grabs the smoking branch. He holds it up to the nest. The smoke clouds the nest, and the humming increases to a dull roar.

"Joseph!" Eliza shouts. "Stop it!"

"Just calm down!" Joseph says, but he also sounds scared.

You scramble to climb down, too frightened of the bees buzzing around your head. But as you reach for a branch, something stings the back of your neck.

"They're stinging me!" you shout.

"Me too!" Eliza and Joseph cry out.

As the three of you tumble to the ground, your eyes feel puffy, and you can't catch your breath. You look down at your fingers and see that they're swelling up.

You have an allergic reaction to the bee stings. Your journey ends here.

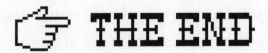 **THE END**

The idea of floating down the rapids on a raft sounds too dangerous to everyone in your family. You decide the Barlow Toll Road sounds safer, even if that means spending the extra money and facing the steep hill. It's worth it to avoid the risk of capsizing into the icy cold waters of the Columbia River. You shiver, remembering how cold you were in the pond you fell into. The last thing you want is anything even remotely close to that dreadful experience.

Most of the families agree and plan to follow the Barlow route and pay the toll at the end. A couple of others decide to risk the rapids. You wish them luck and leave them as they start building rafts. You hope to see them again in Oregon City before too long.

If all goes well on the toll road, you should be in Oregon City in about two weeks. As your family makes its way down the path Barlow carved, the first stop is the Tygh Valley, where you make camp. You have entered the famous Cascade Mountain range now, and the path is steep and treacherous at times.

"The tollgate is coming up," Pa says as you make camp. "We should reach it tomorrow."

As promised, you arrive at Barlow's Gate the next day after a long trek through the mountains. The station there is a welcome change, and Ma is pleased to find fruit available for sale. Your food supplies have slowly been dwindling, and you are down to the basics now. Ma has been careful to make sure everyone gets enough to eat to replenish their energy but nothing extra. She's afraid that you will run out before the journey ends if you have any delays.

"This almost makes paying the toll worth it,"

Ma says with a smile as she shows you the apples she selected. "I'm going to make a pie with these tonight."

The pie is delicious, but it doesn't make up for the grueling travel through the mountains. After hours of climbing, you are hungrier than ever. You pass the time dreaming of the big meals you will enjoy in Oregon City. You know you will sit down to a table loaded with all your favorite foods. It's been nothing but beans, bacon, and pan bread for weeks now.

"We are approaching Laurel Hill," Caleb declares after two more days of exhausting climbs. This is the steep hill you were warned about.

"How in the world will we get down there?" Ma asks, looking at the tremendously sharp descent.

You think back to Alcove Spring, at the beginning of the Trail, where the men of the train used their collective strength to lower the wagons down the challenging incline. That seems like much longer than five months ago. And with everyone as worn out and exhausted as they are, it's probably not a good idea.

"We could lower the wagons with ropes," a woman suggests. "Tie them securely to trees first."

She explains that you would lead the animals down separately, after loading as much as you could onto them.

"Or we could cut some of the biggest trees down and tie them to the backs of the wagons," a man says.

You wonder what that would do.

"The weight of the trees would create enough drag on the wagons to stop them from rolling too quickly and bumping into the animals," he explains.

Both options sound risky. As expected, there are lots of opinions about which to choose, and the debate grows intense. Finally, Caleb makes everyone quiet down.

"We'll vote," he says, "and settle it that way."

There are seven wagons left in your group. Three choose the ropes, and three others choose to cut down the trees.

"Your family is the tiebreaker," Caleb says, turning to Ma and Pa. "What do you want to do?"

If you decide to lower the wagons with rope, turn to page **127**

If you cut the trees and pull them with the wagons, turn to page **131**

You can't imagine turning back at this point. Pa brought you so far, and to return to Kentucky without him would be even more heartbreaking than continuing. You're more determined than ever to make it to Oregon City.

You tell Ma your decision, and she nods. She looks so frail, it frightens you. As it grows later in the day, you hear horses approaching and freeze. You aren't sure whether to run and get Pa's rifle or sit still and wait to see who it is. While you are hesitating, two men become visible.

"You all need some help?" one of them asks. From the looks of them, you guess they are fur traders.

"Yes, please," Ma speaks up before you have a chance. "My husband passed away, and we need help getting to Oregon City. I can pay you."

The men look at each other and then back at Ma.

"Sure, ma'am," the same man says, and then they help you bury Pa, which is the hardest thing you've ever had to do in your life.

Later, you hear the men talking to each other, after they check out your wagon and your animal team. Then they return to you and Ma.

"We'll need a fee of two hundred dollars to get you to Oregon City from here," the man who seems to be in charge says.

Two hundred dollars! You feel yourself get hot with anger. Who has that kind of money to spare? You take Ma aside.

"That is robbery," you whisper. "I think they are taking advantage of us."

"What choice do we have?" Ma says. "I'll give them my jewelry to get us to Oregon City safely."

Pa gave Ma those jewels, and he would want her to have them. But he would also feel more comfortable if you weren't alone on the Trail.

What do you tell the men?

If you say it's a deal, turn to page **118**

If you say you will go on your own, turn to page **120**

Pa looks at you all.

"Are you sure?" he asks.

"Yes," Ma says, speaking for all of you. "We will go down the Columbia River."

You know it isn't an easy thing for Ma to agree to, especially since even simple river crossings have always made her nervous. This is a bit more complicated and potentially more dangerous. But at least this time you will be traveling on a raft. And by taking this route, you can avoid the toll road and the dangers of the Barlow route.

While Pa goes to tell Caleb and the rest of the wagon train about your decision, you check out your surroundings with Joseph and Eliza.

"I wonder why this area is called The Dalles," you say, expecting Joseph to give one of his usual detailed answers. But he just shrugs, and Eliza pipes up instead.

"Pa told me the French named it because of the way the land is shaped like a big trough," she says. "*Dalles* is the word for 'trough' in French."

You imagine explorers coming from as far as France to see what you're looking at now. And here you are, finally on the last part of your journey to Oregon City. Amazing!

When Pa returns, he tells you the plan.

"Only a few of the families are going with us," he explains. "The rest are taking the Barlow Toll Road."

You feel a pang of concern. What if you made the wrong decision?

"But don't worry," Pa continues, as if he is reading your mind. "I'm going to build us a nice strong raft, and we will be fine."

Pa's carpentry skills have been a huge asset on this trip, and once again they will be put to use.

"I'll have to cut down several of those tall trees to start," he tells you. "And then I'll shape them into planks and lash them together to make the raft."

The raft will have to be strong enough to carry your wagon, the animals, and your family down the river. It's a big job, but you're confident Pa can do it. But first, you will all make camp and get a good night's rest.

The next morning, Caleb approaches your family's campfire at breakfast with some news.

"Several men from the nearby Wasco Nation have offered to help us across the river," he says.

"Do they have a ferry?" Pa asks. "I haven't heard of it."

"Not exactly a ferry," Caleb continues. "But they take people across in large canoes."

"Why would we want to do that?" Pa asks. "I'm going to build the raft, which will be big enough for all of us."

"They have a lot of experience with the river, so it might be safer," Caleb says. "But they won't be able to take your whole family at once. You'd have to break up."

Ma and Pa exchange looks. You know they don't like the idea of splitting you up. But traveling on the canoes would mean less weight for the raft to carry. The Wasco people are friendly, Caleb says, but they would need some goods in exchange for their help.

What do you decide?

If you ask the Wasco Nation for help, turn to page 128

If you decide to stick to your own raft, turn to page 105

I don't want you to go," you tell Pa, knowing Ma feels the same.

Pa nods, almost relieved. "I think that's the right choice." He smiles, looking proud. "If we separate, it could be much worse and—"

A cold gust of wind interrupts Pa and pushes a flurry of snow into the wagon train. The temperature dramatically drops, and snow fills the air.

"It's snowing!" yells Hannah, bouncing up and down.

"Bizarre to see snow this time of year," says Caleb, turning to Pa. "I agree that if we get lost, it'll be hard to find our way back to the camp. All this snow doesn't help matters much either."

"Then let's continue on," says Pa. "We'll stay near the camp and hunt."

"Maybe Joseph and I can trap some rabbits," you suggest.

"Good thinking," Pa says.

You shoulder your heavy pack and continue on through the fresh snow, the weight somehow feeling a little lighter knowing that Pa won't be out there on his own, leaving you behind.

Your group has wandered higher into the Blue Mountains, where the trees are sparser and it's easier to navigate. The snow is loose and powdery beneath your feet. Suddenly, you hear something that sounds like thunder overhead. Thunderstorms aren't unheard of in the middle of winter, but this sounds different, closer somehow. It's as if the whole earth is shaking beneath your feet.

"Avalanche!" shouts Caleb. "Try to find cover in the trees!"

But the snow is barreling down too quickly on you and the other families, and the thick trees are too far down the mountain. Chaos overtakes everyone, and all you can see is that white powder crashing down toward you.

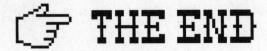 **THE END**

You all agree that the best choice is to go around the dunes, rather than try to pass through them. The wagon train slowly makes its way around the massive mounds of sand. You look up at them, impressed by how winds piled up these huge hills over time, to the point where they stand hundreds of feet high. And even more impressive is how they don't just blow away.

As you hike, Caleb tells everyone that there are

hot springs coming up after a few days' hike, and that perks up the mood a bit. You remember the fun everyone had back at the Soda Springs, where there were geysers and a spring that fizzed and bubbled like soda. That would be refreshing right now!

As you leave the dunes, your wagon train passes several beautiful areas, including a lake and canyons. There's good hunting, too, with plenty of antelope and birds. Caleb halts the wagons every now and then when someone spots a good hunting opportunity.

You're near a canyon, and during the next break, Ma says it's okay to go exploring for a little while. Eliza has always loved to climb, and you scramble up the side of a big cliff with her, ready to see what's at the top.

"Hurry up!" Eliza says, ahead of you. You race after her, happy to feel the breeze on your face. It's a clear, sunny day and one of the nicest you've had in a long time.

When you get to the top of the cliff, the view of the canyon is spectacular.

"Oh, look!" Eliza says, and you turn, expecting her to point out something in the scenery. But instead it's a little kitten, peeking its head out from behind a rock.

"It's so cute," you say with a smile for the orange cat with huge green eyes.

"Here, kitty," Eliza beckons, holding her hand out to the tiny cat. But it just stays where it is, motionless.

"Don't be scared," Eliza continues, taking a few steps closer. "I won't hurt you." She bends, making herself smaller and less threatening.

But when she reaches the kitten and tries to pet it, the frightened cat swats her paw and scratches Eliza on the face. Eliza recoils, covering her cheek, and doesn't watch where she is stepping. She slips and stumbles off the edge of the cliff!

"Eliza!" you shout, imagining your friend

plummeting to the ground, hundreds of feet below. You rush to the edge, terrified, and find Eliza clinging to a rock an arm's length below you.

"Hold on!" you say, your heart racing as you wonder what to do. Do you lean forward and reach out your hand for her to hold on to? Then you can use all your strength to pull her up. Or do you try to find a sturdy branch for her to grab? That might be easier, but it means she will have to wait, and you don't know how long she will be able to hold on. What do you do?

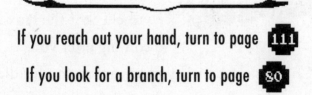

If you reach out your hand, turn to page **111**

If you look for a branch, turn to page **80**

You slowly turn your body away from the lynx, pivoting on your toes so you don't make any sudden moves. Archie is still facing the wildcat, staring at it.

"Okay, Archie, on the count of three, we are going to make a break for it," you say in a whisper.

"One. Two. Three. Let's go, boy!" you shout as you start in a dead sprint toward camp. Archie follows right behind you. Your heart is beating fast, and you're afraid to turn back to check if the lynx is coming after you.

"Come on, Archie!" you scream as you hurdle over small branches that have fallen to the ground. You're churning your legs faster than you ever have before. Suddenly you see Archie stumble in a small ditch.

"Get up!" you shout as Archie twists his body to get back up. But the lynx is on top of him! You watch in horror as the wildcat bites into the side of Archie's neck. His paws swat the lynx in the face, and Archie barks so loudly that it seems to startle the cat. After several more growls, the lynx spots a deer in the distance and takes off after it. You rush toward Archie to help him, and he is whimpering. You lift him into your arms and carry him back to camp. There, the vet bandages up Archie to prevent him from losing more blood.

A few weeks pass, and Archie's wounds have healed, though he doesn't seem quite like himself. You decide to play fetch—maybe that will cheer him up. As you are about to throw the stick, Archie bites down on your arm.

You yell in agony. The vet from camp runs to your side.

"Were you bit?" the vet asks.

"It was just Archie," you explain.

The next day is one of the saddest of your life as you help Pa bury Archie, who, despite all your hopes, died suddenly in the night. You make a marker out of a big stone, and Hannah sprinkles wildflowers on top. You don't want to leave without Archie, but you have to continue, and you leave his grave with a heavy heart and tears in your eyes.

Over the next few days, you have nausea and don't feel like eating anything. Everyone thinks you are just reacting to the death of Archie.

Ma tries to give you some special foods, but you have trouble swallowing, and you start to feel confused. A few days later, you are foaming at the mouth. You die of rabies.

 **THE END**

You pick up the doll and fling it in the direction of the bear. The bear pounces and starts to chew on it while you, Hannah, and Samuel run back to camp. You think you've escaped but then realize that the bear has followed you!

"Run!" you yell to everyone in the camp. "Bear!"

Everyone runs and hides behind a tree. But you watch in horror as the bear ravages your food supply. Ma and Pa had just packed up your food for the remaining oxen to carry. Now the bear feasts on the bacon and sugar and tears through the bags of flour. By the time he finally lumbers away, satisfied, everything is destroyed.

"We're ruined," Ma cries, clutching you as if she doesn't have the strength to stand on her own. "What will we do now?"

You just gulp, speechless. Now you have no wagon

and hardly any food. The rest of the wagon train offers to share what they have, but no one has much extra to spare. They all have to think of their own survival.

Over the next couple of days, your family is forced to kill another one of your oxen for food. When you think about it, you feel sad, but there's no other choice. Even though you were tired of flapjacks, corn cakes, and bacon before, you desperately wish for them now.

As the ox meat runs out, Ma rations meals even more strictly. When you camp, Pa lays traps for small animals, but it's hard to catch anything. You continue to look for berries and fruits with the rest of the kids. But soon the gnawing feeling of hunger starts to become familiar and it's harder to keep walking each day, especially climbing through the mountains.

"I think we should camp for a while so I can try to hunt," Pa says.

"But if we keep going, we might find some food or a trading post up ahead," Ma argues.

"Maybe another train will come by with more food to share," Pa says.

"We can't ask anyone for their food." Ma shakes her head.

"But they might have extra that they are willing to trade with us," Pa replies, trying to sound hopeful.

You listen to your parents debate what to do and try not to feel afraid. Finally, they turn to you.

"What do you think we should do?" they ask.

If you say you should camp, turn to page **26**

If you say you should keep going, turn to page **93**

I'll take care of everything while you're gone if you want to go, Pa," you say, trying to sound brave.

"Thank you," Caleb says to you, with an approving nod. "I think this will be the best bet for everyone."

Caleb, Pa, and a couple of other men from the wagon train take off. As you watch them leave, you feel a little anxious but hopeful that everything will be okay.

That night for supper, Ma fixes small servings of cornmeal hash and beans.

"We need to make this last for as long as we can," she says. You eat your portion and try to tell yourself that you are satisfied as you help do all of Pa's chores.

At night, you wake up to a terrible sound. The oxen are moaning and grunting in a desperate way. You remain in your tent, frozen with fear. Something is attacking them, and it could attack you and your family, too! You have to stay quiet and inside. There's nothing you can do about it.

In the morning, you see that the oxen have been badly injured by some kind of wild animal. They are not going to make it.

Pa returns a few hours later and surveys the dying animals sadly.

"There was no trading post for miles around here," he says. "Maybe if I had been here, I could have saved the oxen."

Your family will continue to push on with what little you can carry on your backs. You take all the food you have, but soon you will run out of food completely.

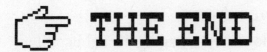 **THE END**

You drop the dirt onto the glowing orange ember and watch it as it turns to black. Then you stomp on the ashes just to make sure the fire is completely out. You've heard of enough fires accidentally burning down camps that you don't want to take any chances. Instead, you go to the wagon and grab one of the quilts that Ma has sewn on the journey. She's made several and has used them to barter for goods along the way. Back in your tent, wrapped snugly in the thick quilt, you're finally able to fall into a deep sleep.

Before you know it, the morning bugle sounds.

"It's already morning?" you mumble as you crawl out of bed, feeling envious that Samuel seems far more rested than you.

You feel like you are dragging as everyone sets out to do the morning chores. Samuel milks Daisy as usual, while Hannah pulls out the dishes for breakfast and grinds coffee. You walk over to the woods to collect firewood, glad that it's so easy to find fuel in this heavily forested area.

Archie follows you, wagging his tail happily.

"*Now* you're with me, instead of last night, when I could have used your help," you say, throwing a small twig, which Archie eagerly runs to fetch and bring back to you.

Playing with Archie wakes you up, and you end up moving a bit farther from camp than you expected. But it feels good to race with Archie in the crisp early-morning air, and you're starting to feel a bit more energized.

"I guess I should start gathering some branches," you finally say aloud. "I don't want to keep breakfast waiting."

Just then, your dog freezes, and you hear a low growl emerge from him.

"What is it, boy?" you ask as you glance around with concern. But you don't see anything alarming nearby.

Archie continues to stare at something and growl. You try to see what is bothering him and squint toward the trees. *Yikes!* Blending in with the branches of a tree is something that makes your heart skip a beat.

It's a lynx! A giant gray lion-like cat is staring straight at you, watching your every move. Its gray eyes are piercing, and its long hair almost forms a beard. Frozen, you stare back at the big cat. You've heard about these beautiful but dangerous creatures, but you have never seen one before in real life.

"Hush, Archie," you whisper softly as your heart races. The cat's ears are twitching, and you wonder if it is feeling threatened by Archie. All its muscles seem tensed, like it might be ready to leap at any second. Is it going to attack you? You know that lynxes move very quickly and are powerful, and you don't want to get in the way of this one's sharp claws.

You try to stay calm and think about what you should do, even as you feel your heartbeat pounding in your throat. Your gut reaction is to run back to camp as quickly as you can, but you don't know if it will chase you. Another option is to try to scare the lynx away by yelling, throwing rocks at it, and waving your arms around. But what if that just makes it angry and encourages it to attack?

What do you do?

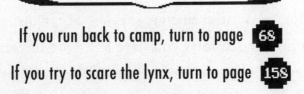

If you run back to camp, turn to page **68**

If you try to scare the lynx, turn to page **158**

Your eyes scan the ground for a branch that is long and strong enough to support Eliza's weight.

"Hold on, Eliza!" you say in a panicked voice, while rifling through several branches. Finally, you find one that should work and run back to where she is still clinging to the rock. The branch extends just far enough for her to grab on to it. With all your might, you are able to pull your friend back up safely.

"Thanks. I thought I was a goner." Eliza gasps, trying to catch her breath. You sit for a few moments, thinking about what could have happened. Then you change the subject, talking about the cat, which has already run away.

"We should get going," you finally say, pulling Eliza to her feet. "Everyone must be waiting for us."

Over the next few days, your wagon train makes its way over to the hot springs. Even though everyone is excited about the change, they are also worried about how much food you have left. Late in your journey, supplies are running low. When you set out from Independence, Missouri, you never thought it

would be possible to run out of bacon, but there isn't even much of that left now.

When you finally arrive at the hot springs, Caleb says you will make camp for a couple of days and rest. Ma is ready to wash your filthy clothes, and all the kids are tasked with helping. As you help Ma scrub while Hannah and Samuel fetch more water, Pa sits down next to both of you and discusses your food situation.

"I'm afraid we're not just running out of food, but we're getting short on supplies, also," Pa says.

"What do you mean?" you ask.

Pa pulls some rope out from his back pocket.

"This is all the rope we have left, and I am not

sure when we are going to get to another trading post for me to get more supplies before Oregon City."

You think about all the ways you use rope on this trip and how important it is.

"I was just asking Ma if I should use what rope we have left to make traps to try to catch some small animals tonight," Pa continues. "Or she could weave it into a fishing net."

The idea of some fresh game or fish makes your stomach grumble. You've gotten good at setting traps with Joseph since the very first time you caught jackrabbits at the beginning of the Trail. But sometimes fish are easier to catch, if it's a good spot on the river. What do you recommend?

If you suggest making traps, turn to page 33

If you suggest making a net, turn to page 95

Joseph, we need to get back," you say. "It's probably time to get rolling again, and we haven't eaten yet."

Joseph looks a little bit annoyed.

"Come on, Joseph," Eliza adds. "The last thing we need is to get stung by bees. You know Pa would be upset if we got hurt."

"I guess you're right," Joseph agrees reluctantly. "I've never actually smoked bees out of a hive before, anyway."

That makes you laugh. Joseph is always filled with facts about everything and knows a lot about all sorts of things. And he also has a lot of good ideas. But sometimes he is a little overconfident, too. You're fine with giving up the honey and heading back to the wagons. Besides, you know that you have Fort Boise to look forward to in the next week. Ma usually lets you get some kind of small treat at the trading posts.

Over the next few days, everyone's patience is tested as the anticipation of getting to Fort Boise grows. You haven't passed a trading post for three weeks!

"I can't wait to get to the fort," Hannah says, walking with you as she swings her worn rag doll by the arm. "I'm going to get a new dress for my doll."

You look at Hannah's own dress and dirty apron and think about the last time you were able to wash your clothes and have a proper bath. You know how raggedy you must look too, just like everyone else in the wagon train.

As you walk, you kick a pebble and notice your dilapidated shoes, which have been repaired several

times already since Ma bought them for you back in Independence. From walking so many miles a day, they are growing paper-thin again and need new soles.

When you finally arrive at Fort Boise, everyone perks up at the welcoming scene. Several other wagon trains are parked in corrals—circles to protect their animals and keep out thieves and predators. There's the bustle of people trading and making repairs to their wagons. People from the Paiute, Nimi'ipuu, and Shoshone Nations offer goods for sale, while kids run around and play.

After you make camp and have supper, Ma gives you permission to explore a little on your own.

"You know this is the last trading post before we get to Oregon City," she says. "This is our last chance to buy anything we need for the rest of the journey. Go look carefully."

You take Samuel and Hannah by the hands and walk around. A group of Nimi'ipuu people have spread out their wares, which include woven blankets, beads, and skins. But as Hannah stops to admire a carved wooden horse, you notice some tall moccasin boots lined with fur.

"These are good for snow," a Nimi'ipuu man says to you.

You politely admire how neatly the leather is stitched and move on.

Another merchant has some rock candy on sticks. The colorful crystals of sugar in jagged shapes form long lollipops. He also has honey candy and molasses for sale that make your mouth water.

When you get back, Ma is discussing what items to get with Pa. She explains that you have enough of the essential foods you need to get to Oregon City. Pa tells her he has completed all the wagon repairs for the rough, rocky, and snowy mountains ahead. And he's purchased any available spare parts.

"We have a little extra money to let the kids get something," she says.

"Can I get the wooden horse toy?" Hannah asks with a pleading look, forgetting about her rag doll's new dress.

"Let's see how much it costs," Pa says with

a smile. Each of you left behind all your toys in Kentucky, and you rarely ask for anything.

"Is there anything you need?" Ma asks you. "If not, I might get us a jar of molasses and extra sugar."

Your mouth starts to water as you think of the molasses. It's been so long since you've had Ma's famous delicious molasses pudding. But you can feel the pebbles underfoot and wonder if you should mention how worn out your shoes are, especially with the hardest part of the mountains ahead of you.

What do you say?

If you say she should get the molasses
and sugar, turn to page **148**

If you say your shoes need repair, turn to page **112**

You can go, but be safe, and we will see you on the other side," Ma says while giving you a hug. Pa places his hand on your shoulder.

"Listen to everything Caleb tells you," he says. You wave goodbye to Samuel, Hannah, and Archie and run back to Caleb with Joseph and Eliza.

"Okay, team, this will be challenging. But if we work together, we should have no problems," Caleb says with a smile. You smile back, then line up next to the animals and help guide them as you start walking.

Your trip around the mountain is difficult. The animals keep trying to veer off the path, and you constantly have to stop and wait for them to line up again. After several hours, you are able to cover some ground.

"I wonder if they are already across and waiting for us," you say to Caleb.

"They should be by now, but they will definitely be there by the time we reach the other side," he replies.

Finally, you are around the mountain and on the

other side of the rapids. You're so excited to tell Pa that you helped save one of the oxen from falling off the side of a cliff. But when you walk around to the mouth of the rapids, no one is there.

"Where are they?" you ask with a sinking feeling.

Caleb looks just as worried as you.

"Let's give them some more time. I'm sure they will be here soon," he replies in a hopeful voice.

You sit staring at the rapids for hours, but there is no sign of your family or anyone else. In the distance, Caleb sees pieces of the raft floating and banging up against the rocks. As night falls, you know that your family is not coming and you are now on your own. Caleb, Joseph, and Eliza try comforting you, but you just want to be alone. You are numb and can't speak. A couple of days later, you have no choice but to continue on with Caleb and his family.

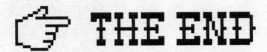 **THE END**

You grab the kettle of warm water and pour it into a bucket. Then you stick your feet inside.

"What are you doing?" Ma asks as she returns with the dishes.

"Look at my feet," you say.

Ma looks at your feet and runs to get the vet, who is the closest thing to a doctor you have in your wagon train.

"It looks like you have a bit of frostbite on your feet," the vet says after taking a look.

"What is going to happen to me?" you ask, feeling scared.

"We'll see," he says. "But you did the right thing to soak your feet in warm water. Do that for a while longer and then wrap them up warmly."

You follow his instructions and in the morning unwrap the blanket covering your feet. Your toes have mostly returned to their normal color, except for the big and pinky toes on both feet. They are an unslightly shade of black.

When the vet sees them, he shakes his head.

"I'm afraid these toes have gangrene. We'll have to remove them so it doesn't spread to the rest of your feet."

You're devastated, but you try to be brave about losing your toes. Ma can't stop crying and seems even more upset than you. Over the next week, she and Pa decide to head south to California. They think it might be an easier trail for you to travel than Oregon. All because of your shoddy shoes, your family's dreams of Oregon are given the boot.

 **THE END**

I think we should keep going," you say, and Ma nods in agreement. "We can still hunt for food, but maybe we will find a trading post."

"I guess you're right," Pa agrees. "But it isn't going to be easy." He gives everyone in the family a load to carry. It's mostly your bedrolls, waterskins, and a few other essential items, but it's still heavy. Pa takes the biggest load for himself, carrying his rifle, ammunition, and camping supplies.

It's hard to keep moving with the bag strapped to your back. You don't want to complain, but your shoulders hurt, and your feet feel like bricks. Plus, you're so hungry that your stomach stops growling and you just feel a hollow pit inside.

Over the next few days, you get weaker and weaker. Finally, you are unable to keep moving. Your family is forced to camp and forage for food in the woods, but you won't find enough to sustain you for much longer.

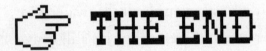 **THE END**

I guess you and Ma agree about the fishing net," Pa says.

You smile and nod.

"I'll finish up the washing if you'll weave me the net," Pa offers Ma. Soon Ma has put together an impressive net.

"This should catch plenty of fish," Pa says, thanking her.

Pa heads toward the river, and you run up behind him. He places his hand around your shoulder, and you walk together to the banks of the river. You grab one side of the net from Pa and fling it into the water.

SPLASH! Your hand accidentally gets stuck in the net, and you fall into the water. You manage to get out of tangle and swim back to the banks with the net, where Pa gives you a hand and pulls you out.

"Let's try that again," Pa says, and you both have a good laugh about what happened.

You throw the net back into the water, and within a couple of hours, you are able to catch several fish for dinner. Ma whips up an amazing supper that leaves you satisfied. Even better, the fiddles come out for the first time in a long while, and everyone enjoys some music and dancing.

A few hours after you eat, you start feeling nauseated and are bent over with pain in your stomach. The night passes and you don't feel any better, spending most of it throwing up.

"I think I know what's wrong with you," Pa says as he sits with you through the night.

"What is it, Pa?" you ask, trying to sound brave.

"You must have swallowed some of the water from the lake, and it's making you sick," he replies. "You'll be fine."

But Pa is wrong. The next few days are very painful, and you don't get any better. You die of dysentery.

 THE END

You choose to ignore Archie's consistent growls and barks. You roll over and gently push him away, hoping to get a little more sleep. But thundering hoofbeats and angry shouts jolt you out of your sleep only a few short minutes later. Scrambling out of the tent, you're horrified to see a gang of bandits surrounding your wagon.

"Hand over all your money and valuables!" the masked leader growls. "Or else!"

Pa, Caleb, and the other families have no choice but to give them what they want. You are forced to give up the rest of your money and what few valuables you have left. The bandits disappear as

quickly as they arrived, leaving you and your family with nothing but the bare essentials in your wagon.

"They must've been watching us, waiting for us to go to sleep so they could strike," Pa says grimly. "No one heard anything?"

You realize with a sinking heart that Archie was trying to warn you about the bandits, but you decided to ignore his warning barks. Now you have no money left for when you get to Oregon. Starting a farm with nothing will be extremely challenging.

"What if we go back to Barlow's Gate and tell the toll operators?" you suggest. "Maybe they could help us catch the bandits."

Pa scratches his head. "That'll cost us days going back. But I suppose we don't have any other options, do we?"

You decide to make the trek back to the tollgate to hopefully get some assistance with the bandits. It's a tiring return journey, especially considering the steep incline of Laurel Hill you now have to climb back *up,* and the oxen grow slower and wearier by the hour. Your whole body aches as you finally make your way back to Barlow's Gate.

But when Pa tells your desperate situation to the toll operators, they are unsympathetic.

"Sorry, folks," one of the operators says, tipping his hat. "That's why you have to be especially careful around these parts. Bandits will snatch the shoes right off your feet if you're not keeping a sharp eye out. Not much we can do about it either."

You know you're never going to get your family's money back. Pa shakes his head, dejected.

You decide to build a small cabin at the base of the valley. Ma will sell pies and blankets to passing travelers, and Pa will hunt and sell furs and dried meat to those in need of supplies and food. It's a meager living, but it's still better than turning back. You can try to save up enough money to make your way to Oregon City next year.

 **THE END**

I think we should keep the wagon," you say.

"Me too," says Hannah. "I love the wagon."

"And I love all our food," Samuel adds.

Ma laughs. "I agree with the kids," she says. "We've come too far and carried our belongings for far too long to give them up now. And even though it's been slow going, we are still making progress."

"I think you're right," Pa says. "It would make me nervous to leave the wagon behind too."

You see the same relief you are feeling on the faces of Hannah and Samuel. The wagon has become your

traveling house away from home, and it feels wrong to give it up unless you absolutely have to.

Everyone else in your wagon train makes the same decision as your family. They agree that if you all work together, you can manage to clear the Trail and keep the wagons rolling, even if it is difficult. Besides, with all this practice, the team is getting faster at clearing away fallen trees. If it reaches a point where it becomes impossible, then you can consider abandoning the wagons. But not yet.

As you hike, you realize that even though the mountainous terrain is challenging, it is also beautiful. With all the tall trees, cliffs, canyons, and purple haze of snowcapped mountains in the distance, the views have been breathtaking.

As you're walking, the wind suddenly begins to blow and the temperature drops.

"That's a northern wind," Ma says, looking concerned.

"Look!" Samuel shouts. "It's snowing!"

Sure enough, flakes of snow fill the air. They land

on your arms and face. You open your mouth and feel the icy coldness melt on your tongue.

"It tastes sweet," you say, laughing. You haven't seen snow for so long, but it feels funny to see it now, when it's still only September.

Archie runs back and forth and barks at the flakes. Hannah just twirls, letting her apron fill with the white fluff.

But within minutes, the light snowfall turns into a fierce storm. The driving winds and thick sheet of white snow are hard to move through. And the animals seem to be scared as the icy cold air pelts their skin. They push against their yokes and kick as if they want to run away.

"Halt the wagons!" Caleb orders.

You watch as everyone huddles together, discussing what to do.

"Do you think we should take cover and make camp," Caleb asks, shouting over the wind, "and wait for the storm to pass?"

"Look at the animals," Pa says. "They might freeze

if we leave them standing in the cold. We need to keep them moving."

"In this?" Ma argues. "We can barely make out where we are going. We can just cover the animals with blankets."

"But maybe if we keep moving, we'll make it out of the storm area," another woman adds.

Back and forth they argue. You don't know which sounds like the best option. Part of you wants to camp, and you hope that you and your friends will be allowed to play in the snow. But you wonder if the arguments for moving forward make sense too.

What does everyone decide?

If you decide to make camp, turn to page 41

If you decide to keep moving, turn to page 35

I think we can manage on our own," Pa says, looking confident. "The raft I'm going to build will be so solid, it'll be like a boat."

After two days of working, the raft is finally ready. As always, you're impressed by Pa's craftsmanship.

Finally, the time arrives to load up the raft. Pa sets it in the water and ties it to the banks with thick ropes. He leads the animals and the wagon onto it, and it stays steady. Then he takes Ma and Hannah by the hand and seats them in the wagon. You and Samuel join them. When everything seems secure, Pa jumps onto the raft and cuts the ropes. You're off!

Pa has big poles he's using to steer the raft. He gives you a second one to help him, since you are the eldest and because you are the strongest swimmer in the family. It makes you feel important to hold the pole and help Pa. And it's fun to be on the river, floating along.

You travel for about an hour with no problem until suddenly the rapids grow faster and the water gets choppier. Pa struggles to keep the raft steady as it lurches in the water, and you try to help. But your pole snaps in half as you plunge it into the water.

"Hold on!" Pa shouts as the raft starts to rock violently. You feel your breakfast start to come up into your throat as you hold on to the wagon for dear life. But once the raft capsizes, you aren't able to grab on to anything and are flailing in the freezing water. You try to swim for shore, but you don't see anything, and your body starts to give out, exhausted.

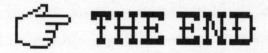 **THE END**

I think I should stay with my family," you respond. "If that's okay."

"No problem. We'll see you on the other side," Joseph says with smile.

You help Pa and some of the other men pull the raft out of the water and carry it to the mouth of the rapids. The path to get there isn't very long, but it's really slippery and narrow. You make your way slowly behind the raft, but you find it hard to keep your footing. Suddenly you hear a muffled shout as Samuel clings to your leg. He is dangling off a steep cliff that sits on the edge of the path!

You extend your hand to pull him up, but in the process, you slip yourself. Your hands are grabbing for anything to hold on to, but the ground is so wet that you slide down the side of the mountain.

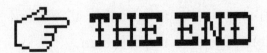 **THE END**

I think we should try the South Alternate Route," you finally say. "It seems like it will be a good choice. And I don't want to cross that river again either."

Ma gives you a grateful smile.

"Okay, it's settled, then," Pa says. "I'll tell Caleb and see what everyone else has decided."

Pa comes back and lets you all know that the other families are going to join you on the route.

"They feel the same way about the river," he says with a smile. "And I can't say I blame anyone."

You set off toward the south and hike without any problems for the first two days. By the third day, it gets drier and dustier, and you are disgusted as you pass the rotting carcasses of a dead ox and horse. There are flies hovering around them, and you cover your mouth and nose with your shirt to block the stench.

"Will that happen to our animals?" a horrified Samuel asks you as you hurry past them.

"I don't know, Sam," you reply. You don't add what else you are thinking: that you don't know what

happened to the people who were with those animals either.

The next day you see something that takes your breath away. Enormous mountains made out of sand are spread out in front of you.

"Whoa. What are those?" Hannah asks, pointing.

"Those are the Bruneau Dunes," Caleb says. "They are made entirely of sand."

"Are we going to have to go all the way around them?" Samuel grumbles. He's been in a bad mood for the past few days, and his face is flushed as he frowns.

"Yes, unless we decide to go through them," Caleb says. "We can try that, because it will save us a day's travel at least. But it will be a challenge."

You gaze up at the massive piles of sand as everyone votes on which way to go. When it is your family's turn, what do you choose?

If you choose to go around the dunes, turn to page **63**

If you choose to go through the dunes, turn to page **30**

You lean forward and stretch out your arm as much as you can toward Eliza.

"Grab my hand!" you shout.

"I can't!" Eliza says. "I'll fall."

"No, you won't," you promise. "I'll pull you up."

"I'm scared," Eliza says, her face red from the exertion of holding on.

"Just try," you say. "Come on, Eliza! Grab on!"

Eliza finally lets go and manages to grab your hand. You hold on tight and try to pull her up with all your strength. But it feels impossible.

"Come on," you groan, pulling harder. Only instead of Eliza coming any farther up, you are pulled down! You try to grab on to something with your feet to stop yourself from sliding over the side of the cliff. But the force of gravity is too strong, and the next thing you know, you are tumbling down the side of the cliff with Eliza behind you.

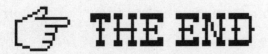 **THE END**

I think I need to get my shoes repaired again," you say, showing Ma how worn-out the bottoms have gotten. She gasps and covers her mouth in surprise.

"I'm so glad you said something!" she says. "How did your shoes wear out so quickly? The cobbler back at Fort Hall must not have done a good job."

"Yes," says Pa, shaking his head. "And we paid him good money, too. Your feet would have frozen while we traveled through these mountains."

Ma goes to look for some buckskin to repair your shoes. But soon she returns instead with the very same moccasin boots you had seen earlier, along with the wooden horse for Hannah and a miniature bow and arrow for Samuel.

"Try these on," Ma says, handing you the boots.

Slipping your foot inside, you're surprised by how light but sturdy they are.

"Are they comfortable?" Ma asks you, and you nod.

"Thank you," you say, thrilled to be out of your uncomfortable shoes.

You feel a mix of emotions on leaving the fort. The next time you will see civilization, it will be in Oregon City. And, as Caleb reminds you, you still have to walk more than 450 miles until you get there.

After a week and a half of hiking, your wagon train reaches what is known as Farewell Bend, where you will forever part ways with the Snake River.

"Even though it brought us challenges, I, for one, will be sorry to say goodbye to this river," Ma says. You wonder if she is thinking of the fresh fish or the water for the animals. It was hard enough crossing the river once; never mind multiple times.

"Are you feeling all right?" you ask, noticing that Ma looks a bit pale.

"I'm fine, dear," she says with a small smile. "My head is feeling a bit heavy is all."

You notice that Ma continues to look weaker over the next day, and she has to stop frequently because her stomach is unwell. At night, when you make camp, she asks you to take charge of making supper.

"I just need to lie down for a bit, and I'll be better," she says.

Pa builds a campfire, and you pull out the skillet and prepare beans flavored with bacon. You try to make Ma's cornbread, too, but it turns out like mush.

You notice Pa picking at his plate.

"I'm sorry the food isn't as good as Ma's," you say, a lump forming in your throat.

"No, no, it's delicious," Pa says, giving you a weak smile. "I'm just not feeling too hungry."

You hope Ma is better tomorrow, because nothing seems right with her sleeping at suppertime instead of being with the rest of you. But the next morning, she isn't better. And, even worse, Pa is sick too. Both your parents just lie in their tent instead of taking part in the usual morning routine.

"I'm sorry, kids," Pa says weakly from his feather mat. "We were both sick all night. We need to rest."

When it's time to roll the wagons, Caleb finds that your family isn't ready to leave yet.

"What's the matter?" he asks you with a frown.

You tell him about Ma and Pa, and he comes back with the man in your wagon train who is a vet. He has been serving as the doctor on your journey. The man goes into their tent and comes out looking grim.

"I'm afraid this is dysentery," he says. "Your parents need rest and plenty of fluids, and hopefully they will pull through."

The lump is back in your throat, and you swallow hard.

"What about the Trail?" you finally manage to ask, noticing how tiny your voice sounds.

Caleb gives you a sad look.

"I'm afraid I can't keep the rest of the wagon train waiting too long. I think I can convince everyone to camp for an extra day, though."

You just nod, grateful. Caleb gives you a pat on the back and hurries back to tell the rest. You spend the day trying to get your parents to eat or drink, but they can't manage to keep much down.

That evening, you peek into your parents' tent again.

"The wagon train is getting ready to roll out tomorrow," you say. "Are you going to be okay to go?"

"Do you think you can drive the oxen team?" Pa asks you. "We don't have the strength to walk, but Ma and I can ride in the wagon."

"But if you don't feel comfortable," Ma adds, "we can just wait until we are better to travel. We'll be able to move faster and can catch up with the rest of the train later."

You think about what both your parents say. As much as you like the idea of taking charge and leading the wagon yourself, it also makes you nervous. Already, it's been tough to be in charge and take care of everything on your own. Maybe a little more rest here, by the river, will be better for everyone. But you also hate the idea of being left behind.

What do you decide?

If you decide to steer the oxen and head out, turn to page **122**

If you decide to stay camped a little longer, turn to page **23**

"kay, mister," you say reluctantly. "We don't have the money, but we have jewelry."

"I need to see it first," the man says as he coughs. "And we take half now, and the rest when we get to Oregon City."

You dig Ma's jewelry box out from the fabric-lined chest in the wagon that holds all your family's valuables and give it to Ma. The men take the jewels Ma offers them. You see one of them eyeing her wedding ring.

"This one I keep," she says firmly.

Even though you don't want to admit it, it's a relief to have the men's help. They help you pack up the wagon and cut wood for the campfire. You didn't realize how exhausted you were from doing your chores and Pa's, plus taking care of Ma.

But over the next couple of days, you start to feel weak, and by the third, you are riding in the wagon with Ma. You have caught a cold and soon you will follow Pa to his grave.

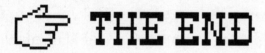 **THE END**

That's okay, mister," you tell the man, standing as tall as you can. "I'm going to get my family to Oregon City on my own."

The men start to snicker softly, and you feel your face burn.

"Suit yourself," the leader finally says. "Good luck to you. And sorry for your loss."

Ma thanks them for their help, and they ride off. She tries to give you an encouraging nod and then goes to lie down in the wagon. You pack up the rest of your family's things with Samuel and Hannah and start the wagon rolling.

As you travel farther into the Blue Mountains, you try to hold on to the determined feeling that keeps you going. But as the days go by, Ma still isn't strong enough to walk. And you find the Trail almost impossible to navigate, with large trees blocking the path. You can't cut them up and move them on your own.

"What's that?" Samuel asks, pointing toward what looks like a little cottage nestled among the trees.

It's a small abandoned log cabin! You decide to stay in the cozy space for a while and give Ma time to heal. You learn how to set traps and hunt so you can feed your family through the long, cold winter. All the while, you think of Pa and what he would want you to do. That makes it easier. When spring comes around, you promise yourself, you'll find a way to continue on your journey somehow.

 **THE END**

I can steer the wagon so we don't fall behind," you say, trying to sound surer of yourself than you feel.

"I think that's a good decision," Pa says with a proud look on his face.

"I agree," Ma says. "It actually might not have been safe to stay here alone."

The next morning, you, Samuel, and Hannah break up your camp and pack up the wagon the best you can, with some help from the others. You lay Ma and Pa's feather mats in the back, after rearranging things to make it less lumpy.

Caleb helps Ma climb into the wagon and then turns to you.

"We're going to be approaching the Blue Mountains soon. It's good your family isn't staying behind," he says in a hushed voice. "I'd hate to think of what would happen to you if your parents took a turn for the worse."

You just nod. That was something you've been trying not to think about. Although this trip has been filled with challenges, you have never been as scared as you are now. You've heard stories of orphans along the Trail who have to either continue on their own or depend on the generosity of others. It makes your stomach turn, and you try to push the thought out of your head.

"I'll send Joseph and Eliza to help you out throughout the day," Caleb continues. "And if you need anything, just shout."

You nod again and take a deep breath before starting the oxen moving.

I have to push on, you tell yourself. *I have to get my family to Oregon City.*

You've passed Farewell Bend now, and Snake River is behind you. As your wagon train has to cut its way through shoulder-tall sagebrush, the journey is slow and exhausting. Up ahead are the famous Blue Mountains, filled with woods and steep climbs. You desperately hope Ma and Pa are better soon. Hannah and Samuel are as helpful as they can be, tending to Ma and Pa and listening to you without arguing. You see both of them wipe back tears when no one is looking, and you know how hard they are trying to be brave, because you feel exactly the same way.

Over the next couple of days, you are relieved when Ma and Pa do start to improve. By the fourth day, Pa is walking next to you again, and Ma is sitting up in the wagon and smiling. You feel lighter, like a huge load has been lifted off your shoulders.

⭐ ⭐ ⭐

Look at those trees!" Samuel says, grinning widely as he runs up to you. "They must be more than two hundred feet tall!"

You've passed Flagstaff Hill and are now in the Blue Mountains. You stretch your neck upward to look at the massive fir trees around you. Like everyone, you've never seen anything like them before.

"I think you're right, Sam," you say, grabbing your brother and tickling him. "Let's see if you can climb to the top of one."

"You first!" Sam says, wiggling out of your reach and running away.

Archie seems amazed by the landscape too and runs ahead of you, sniffing at the ground and chasing birds. Even though it's only September, high up in the mountains, in the shade of the trees, the air has a chill to it. You look forward to making camp and sitting by the fire.

Ma fixes a nice supper, and you're glad to taste her cooking again. Even though no one complained when you were making supper, you know everyone else is happy too. When you are all done eating and talking about the day, someone pulls out a fiddle and starts singing. This kind of night is your favorite, as Samuel and Hannah start to dance and everyone claps. Finally, Ma puts out the fire, and you head to

bed. But as you lie on your feather mat, you can't fall asleep. You're thinking about all that has happened over the past week. Plus, you just can't get warm.

Archie is curled up in a ball next to Samuel, and you wish he were lying next to you instead. But then your brother would be cold. You pass Hannah, holding her doll tight and shivering underneath her blanket, as you head out of the tent to look for an extra blanket in the wagon.

Passing by the campsite, you notice an ember glowing faintly in the fire pit. You start to pick up a handful of dirt to smother it out, then pause. You wonder if you should add a few sticks to get a flame going and sit by it a bit longer to warm yourself up. Or should you just put it out and try to find another blanket and go back to bed?

If you smother the fire, turn to page **76**

If you build a small fire to warm yourself, turn to page **39**

I sure hope these ropes hold," Pa says.

You tighten the last rope from the tree to the side of the wagon. Pa carefully pushes the wagon to the edge. As the wagon makes its way down the steep incline, you hear the tree make a cracking sound. The weight of the wagon is making the tree bend forward.

Pa is looking down the side to make sure that the wagon stays straight and doesn't bang into the side of the mountain. You call out to him, but he doesn't respond. After several more attempts, he finally turns around and sees the tree. Almost immediately the tree snaps in half and goes whizzing by your face down the side of the mountain.

CRASH! You hear the loudest sound of your life. You walk over to the edge to look and see your wagon, smashed to bits and pieces. Your chances of making it Oregon have been crushed with it.

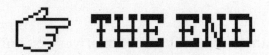 **THE END**

You accept the Wasco people's offer to be canoed down the Columbia River. One of the men introduces himself as Tsuk as he shakes hands with Pa. They decide that Pa will take the wagon and the animals on the raft, while the rest of you will have Tsuk take you to the other side.

"It's better to be safe than sorry," Pa says. "Even though I know my raft would do the trick," he adds with a wink.

Ma and Samuel make it across the river first and are waiting for you and Hannah on the other side

when you step into the canoe, accepting the hand
Tsuk holds out for you. The ride is smooth and swift,
and as you approach the banks of the river, Pa is
already moving the wagon off the raft and speaking
to Caleb about how to get across the Cascade Rapids,
up ahead. You thank Tsuk for the canoe ride, then
huddle up by Caleb, who gathers everyone together
and tells you the plan.

"I will take all the animals around the south side
of the mountain and meet you on the other side of

the rapids. It's too dangerous for us to put everything on the raft and try to get across," Caleb says.

Everyone agrees. The wagons are lined up, and Caleb ties the final ropes to attach the animals together. Joseph and Eliza run over to you as some of the families make their way onto the rafts.

"Why don't you come with us?" Joseph says. "We could use another hand."

Do you ask Ma and Pa to go with them, or do you stick with your family?

If you ask to go with Joseph's family, turn to page 88

If you say you want to stay with your family, turn to page 107

You decide that while both options are risky, weighing the wagons down with heavy logs still sounds like a better option. The ropes might not be able to hold the weight of the heavy wagons and snap, which would be disastrous. Your family votes to cut down logs rather than attempt lowering the wagons.

"I agree," says Caleb. "I think the incline is too steep to try something like that here. That, and I don't know if we'd all have the strength to lower even one wagon. If one of us gives out, we're sunk. Let's stop for a while to catch our breath, then cut down a couple of these enormous trees to drag behind the wagons."

You're glad for the chance to rest, however short it may be. You, Joseph, and Eliza make a game out of picking out the tallest trees in sight and imagining how long it would take you to climb up to the top branches.

Pa, Caleb, and the others cut down several hefty trees and tie the logs up to the backs of the wagons. Still, it's going to be a treacherous descent, and the oxen are already tugging at their ropes.

Slowly but surely, the wagons descend the steep incline of Laurel Hill. The trek down is rocky, slipperier than you imagined, covered with moss and wet leaves, and more than a little frightening. But the trees dragging behind the wagons help to keep everything from careening down the hill. The oxen resist the steep incline initially, but eventually you and Pa help calm them down enough to carefully lead them down to the bottom.

Although your legs are hurting and tired from balancing your own trek down the slope, you can see the valley stretching out ahead. The landscape beyond is unlike anything you've ever seen—covered with lush grass meadows, mossy nooks, and thick pine trees rising into the distance. You think you see something misty obscuring the trees—maybe smoke from a nearby campfire, but you're moving too quickly, and you dismiss it as just a wisp of cloud.

"We did it!" you cheer as Archie barks in excitement. You, Joseph, and Eliza exchange relieved grins.

Caleb finally gives the order to camp for the night, and despite exhaustion, everyone's spirits are high. You and Joseph trap a few rabbits hiding among the trees. You bring them back to Ma, and she cooks up a hearty rabbit stew, along with the usual beans and pan bread. You're bone-weary but relieved that the worst of the mountain journey seems to be behind you. Oregon City is so close, you can almost see it through the thick trees.

But as you drift off to sleep, Archie's barking wakes you up. You groan and try to roll over, but then you feel teeth digging into your clothes. Archie tries to pull you off your bedroll and drag you outside the tent.

"Get off, Archie!" you grumble, wiggling away. "What's the matter with you?"

Archie bolts outside the tent, still barking wildly. When he pulls at your clothes again, you finally peer outside. Even with your bleary-eyed vision, you don't see anything out of the ordinary.

"Be quiet, Archie!" you order. "There's nothing out there!"

But he continues to bark.

With a groan, you eventually clamber out of your tent. Archie wouldn't just be barking like this for nothing. Maybe, just to be safe, you should ask someone on watch. You find the guard near one of the wagons, adding another log to the dying fire.

"I haven't seen anything," he says with a shrug. "Maybe your dog just smelled a skunk nearby."

"Maybe," you say doubtfully. Archie's ears are pricked, and his nose twitches. There could be a more dangerous animal around, but with someone on guard duty, you feel more at ease.

But Archie tugs on your clothes again and keeps barking. It looks like he's trying to lead you somewhere. But where? You hesitate. Should you see where he's trying to lead you?

If you follow Archie to see where he takes you, turn to page **163**

If you ignore him and try to sleep, turn to page **97**

You try your best to make your way over to the darker spot under the ice. Your clothes are feeling heavy and are weighing you down. The water is freezing, and with every stroke that you make to get closer to the darker spot, it feels like you have used all your energy. A little bubble of air escapes your mouth, and you know that you're running out of time.

The sound of voices is coming through the ice, and you can't really tell what is being said, but you know it must be Joseph and Samuel. Finally, you reach the spot of ice you were swimming toward. You try to push up against the ice and punch a hole in it. Another little bubble of air escapes your mouth. For a second, everything seems dark, and then you try pushing up on the ice again. But nothing is working!

Joseph's voice is getting louder, and you can make out what he is saying.

"Tap on the ice so I know where you are!" Joseph shouts.

With all your strength, you try to push up on the ice, but it just won't budge. You keep punching and pounding on the ice, but it remains solid as steel.

"Help!" you scream under the water, and all the air escapes your mouth.

Your arms are getting tired and you keep trying to kick with your legs, but you are sinking farther down, away from the ice. You reach out your arms, but you have sunk too far down.

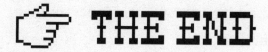 **THE END**

I think it makes more sense to stick with the Trail," you say after thinking it over. "The dunes sound a little scary to me."

"What do you think?" Pa asks Ma and Hannah. "Can you handle more river crossings?"

"We'll have to," Ma says, while Hannah nods her head bravely. "It's more feasible than the dunes." She sighs. "It'll be good practice for the Columbia River, ahead."

"It's settled, then," Pa says. "I'll tell Caleb what we have decided."

The rest of the wagon train agrees with you,

except for a couple of folks, and they don't take much convincing. At this point, no one in the group wants to split up unless there is absolutely no other choice. There's safety in numbers, and as things get harder along the Trail, you have to work together as a team to survive.

The first time you cross Snake River again, you help Caleb and Pa tie the wagons together in order to float them across the river. The current is strong, and you worry you'll lose oxen in the water, but everyone makes it without a hitch.

After trekking aggressively for a day and a half, you reach the next Snake River crossing. Everyone decides to rest for a few hours before facing the river again.

I t's time to rally!" says Pa as he grabs a tool to fasten the wagon wheels.

The cold water shocks the oxen, and they buck when they enter the water.

Caleb's face screws up with concern. "They're going to break an axle!" he shouts.

An ox breaks out of the yoke and floats adrift down the river. No one is able to swim fast enough to catch it. The axle is broken too.

You finally get everyone across the river, and you're thankful you didn't lose more than one ox as Pa replaces the broken axle.

You fall back into the routine of hiking for the next few days, heading north toward the Boise River, a tributary of the Snake River. The dusty trail is filled with sage bushes and not much else. Along the way, you spot more tombstones and simple grave markers of unlucky pioneers who have traveled before you but not made it. Some are proper gravestones etched with people's names, while others are just piles of rocks.

The graves that look like they have been there for a while have weeds growing around them. Others are fresher, more recently dug. You notice one covered with a thick layer of rocks to keep coyotes and other animals from digging up whoever lies there. It makes you shudder.

"'Here lies Bill. He didn't make it up the hill,'" Joseph says after seeing your expression, pretending to read from the gravestone of a man named William Smith.

"Is that really what it says?" Samuel asks, since he is still learning how to read.

"Yes," Joseph says, winking at you. You smile back. Your friend can always make jokes to lighten the mood.

After you've been hiking for several miles along the dusty trail, the mountains to your right and the rock bank to your left start to recede. A green valley suddenly comes into view.

"This is Bonneville Point," Caleb says with a flourish of his hand. "And that is the Boise River Valley."

Everyone is thrilled to see green grass for the first time in so long.

"Look at the trees," Ma says, pointing toward them with a smile. "This is nice."

The next day, as you enter into the valley, Caleb halts the wagons early for your midday break and gives you some extra time to rest.

"Can we go play for a little while?" you ask Ma as she prepares a snack for the family with leftovers from breakfast.

"Yes," she agrees. "But don't go too far, and don't delay coming back."

"Let's race over there!" Eliza points toward a few trees in the distance, and suddenly your tired legs are reenergized. You dash off toward the trees, with Joseph close behind you.

"I'm going to beat you all to the top," Eliza challenges, starting to climb a tree. You are always impressed with Eliza's ability to run, jump, and climb. Before you know it, she is halfway up the tree, and you start to climb after her.

As you reach into the branches to get higher, you hear a buzzing sound. Alarmed, you look around, but it's just some honeybees. Then you notice a beehive hanging from a branch above you, and your heart starts to beat faster.

"*B-b-bees,*" you tell your friends in a hushed voice.

"Get down," Eliza says, quickly making her way down the tree. "You don't want to get stung."

"Wait! Let's smoke out the bees first and get the honey," Joseph says.

"What do you mean?" you ask, shrinking away from the hive.

"We'll get the bees to leave their nest, and cut out some of the honeycomb to eat," Joseph explains, getting excited.

"But isn't that dangerous?" you ask, eyeing the bees suspiciously.

"No," Joseph says. "I know what I'm doing, and I'll do it. And besides, can't you already taste the honey?"

You imagine delicious, sweet honey, dripping off the honeycomb. You haven't tasted anything new for weeks now, and it is tempting to think of spreading the honey on your leftover cornbread from this morning. But you're a little nervous about getting stung by a bee, which has never happened to you before. Plus, Ma told you not to be gone for too long.

What do you say to Joseph?

If you agree to collect the honey, turn to page **46**

If you tell Joseph you want to go back, turn to page **83**

You think about everything until your head starts to hurt, and you still don't know what to do. Then you look over at Ma and your siblings. It looks like they are broken, and you feel the same on the inside. You can't imagine them pushing on any farther on the Trail, at least not right now. Ma is still so weak, and now with Pa gone, you worry if she will continue to get better, or . . . you can't even think about it.

Samuel helps you dig a grave for Pa. He puts on his bravest face and cries as he works the ground. You think about how the shovel you are using was meant for the new farm your family was supposed to have in Oregon, and your tears fall onto the dirt. But you dig the deepest grave you can so no animals can get to Pa's body. And then you cover the dirt mound with as many rocks as you can find. Finally, you scratch Pa's initials and the date onto a big flat rock and use it as a tombstone.

Ma watches you and Samuel work and holds tight to Hannah. When you tell her your decision to go back to Fort Boise, she just nods absently, staring at

Pa's grave. You follow her eyes and wonder if you are thinking the same thing. *Will I ever come back here to visit Pa again?*

As you leave the campsite, heaviness settles over your heart, and your throat tightens up. You scatter a handful of wildflowers over Pa's grave and then don't turn around again. You're not sure how you manage, but soon you lead your family back to the fort. There you find a kind fur trader who says you are welcome to make camp and stay for as long as you need. Over the next month, he gives you small jobs, helping outfit pioneers who pass through for the mountains.

You resole shoes, sell Ma's quilts and pies, and help find guides for those who need them.

As time goes by and you hear the stories and dreams of other families, you realize that you don't want to go back to Kentucky. The Trail is a part of your life now, and it's the dream Pa wanted for you. Even if it wasn't meant to happen now, you'll try again to get to Oregon City next year.

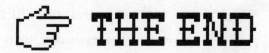 **THE END**

That sounds sweet," Pa says with a grin as you tell Ma she should get the goodies for the family.

Ma comes back with jars of sweet molasses and a sack of sugar. Your family leaves the fort in a good mood and continues up the side of the mountains. Like everyone else, you start off feeling refreshed, but after a few days, you have trouble keeping up. It seems with every step you take, you feel more and more of the ground beneath you, and it hurts.

"Is everything okay?" Joseph falls back and asks you.

"My feet are killing me," you respond. You lift up your shoe to show Joseph.

"I can almost see through to your socks!" Joseph cries. "Why didn't you get your shoes fixed when we stopped?"

You hang your head. "I know. I should've told Ma that I needed new shoes when we were at Fort Boise."

"I have an extra pair of socks," Joseph offers. "Do you want to borrow them?" You thank Joseph but really don't want to wear his smelly socks. *I'll be okay,* you think.

A blanket of white snow is covering the ground ahead, and as you continue up the side of the mountain, the snow is getting deeper. At first you can feel the icy wetness seeping into your shoe, and it makes your sock damp and uncomfortable. But after some hours of walking, you don't even notice it anymore.

When you finally stop to make camp for the night, you sit for a moment and look down at your feet. Your toe is poking out from the front of one shoe, and you find it strange that you didn't even feel it. You untie your shoe and pull off your sock. Your toes are a strange shade of purple and green. *Yuck!* You've never seen anything like it.

You head over to the campfire that Ma has gotten started and sit down with your feet as close to the flames as possible. Ma isn't in sight, and you know she must have gone to gather dishes from the wagon.

You see the kettle for heating water on the fire and have a thought. Should you use some of the heated water to soak them for a little bit? Or should you just sit by the fire and rub your toes to get them back to their normal color?

If you soak your feet in the warm water, turn to page 91

If you rub your feet in front of the fire, turn to page 21

Hannah!" you shout. "Run! Bear!"

Hannah looks up, and horror fills her face. She lets go of her apron, and all the berries tumble onto the ground. And then, without turning around, she starts to run toward you.

You race back to camp, with Samuel two paces ahead of you both. Even though you want to look behind you to make sure the bear isn't following you, you don't. Instead, you just keep running.

Suddenly your foot strikes a big rock in the ground. It sends you flying in the air, and you land hard on the back of your head and are knocked out.

The next thing you know, you are lying on your back, inside your tent. Ma is leaning over you.

"You hit your head," she says, wiping her eyes. "How are you feeling now?"

"I'm okay," you start to say, trying to sit up. But

you are struck with a wave of dizziness and feel like you are going to vomit.

"Lie back down," Ma says.

You fall asleep and don't wake for a long time. Someone tries to shake you, but you can't bring yourself to open your eyes. When you finally do, you see someone but can't recognize who it is.

"Who are you?" you ask. "What am I doing here?"

"I'm your mother," the woman answers. "How are you feeling, my dear?"

You stare at the woman speaking to you but still don't recognize her.

"Where am I?" you ask.

"We are on our way to Oregon," the woman says, while a man rushes into the tent and starts to speak.

It's all making you terribly tired to listen to them trying to tell you who you are and what is happening. You close your eyes. And never open them again.

 **THE END**

You move toward the lighter spot in the ice, which means there is no snow on top of it. Carefully, you swim toward the spot, until you see sunlight. It's the hole! You stick out your head and take in a deep breath of air, trying not to gasp. The calmer you stay, the more likely you will get out alive. So you tread water for the next minute, trying to think about what to do.

"Help me!" you try to shout as you look around for anyone who can pull you out. But your voice is hoarse and comes out only as a whisper. Samuel is nowhere in sight. You are on your own.

You find the thickest piece of ice on the side to hold on to and slowly lift yourself halfway out of the water, leaning on your elbows. You're nervous you'll break the ice again and end up back in the water. Gently, you lean forward and kick your feet to help push yourself. You slowly make your way out, then lie on the ice and snow, panting, exhausted, and shivering.

Standing back up could mean falling through the

ice again, so instead you roll toward the edge of the pond. Finally, when you're sure it's safe, you get on your knees and stand up on firm ground. *Phew!*

You're numb from the cold but run back to camp. When you get there, Ma gasps when she sees you drenched and shivering. She grabs you and orders you to take off all your wet clothes. Then she brings you dry ones, wraps you in a blanket, and sits you in front of the fire.

"Thank goodness you got out of there," she cries, holding you tight and trying to warm you as you tell her and Pa what happened.

"You did everything right," Pa says. "That was extremely dangerous, and you could have been trapped . . ."

Pa's voice gets choked up, and he can't finish his sentence. Instead, he just shakes his head as if he's pushing out the thought, gives you a quick hug, and fixes you a steaming mug of hot coffee to drink.

Your family is back on the Trail the

next morning. It was a close call, but for now it seems like you escaped your fall into the icy pond without getting hurt or sick.

The next several days are uneventful as you make your way through the mountains. Everyone is getting increasingly excited as the end of your journey is becoming more of a reality. You are only a few weeks away from Oregon City!

Your wagon train has finally reached an area known as The Dalles, which you've been hearing about for weeks. It's where the Columbia River sinks into an area filled with massive boulders. Up until a couple of years ago, all pioneers had to travel down the swift river rapids on rafts they built themselves. But ever since a man named Samuel Barlow built a new road to the south that goes around Mount Hood, there's another option too.

"This might be the biggest decision of our trip," Ma says, staring at the rushing rapids with you. "Do we travel down this or go around it?"

"Why wouldn't we just go around?" you ask.

"Well, the Barlow Road costs five dollars a wagon, and we don't have much money left," Ma explains. "And it has its own challenges, including a very steep hill."

Another steep hill! None of the others you've encountered on the Trail have been easy. And five dollars is a lot of money, which you'll need to start your farm. But the rapids look equally dangerous, like they could easily flip a raft. You hear everyone

debating the pros and cons of each. Not everyone has enough money left for the toll. In the end, they agree that every family must choose the route that it feels most comfortable taking. What does yours decide?

If you pay the five-dollar toll, turn to page **48**

If you risk the rapids, turn to page **56**

Shoo!" you shout, waving your arms around. The big cat continues to stare at you, muscles tensed, without blinking. You steel your nerves and fight the urge to run. Instead you pick up the biggest stone you can find. Flinging it in the direction of the lynx, you continue to yell at it.

"Go on, now!" you shout. "Go!"

Archie starts to bark at the lynx too. Together, the two of you make such a ruckus that the lynx finally turns its head and slinks away.

You breathe an enormous sigh of relief and realize you are drenched in sweat.

"Come on, Archie," you say, grabbing a few branches for the fire. You race back to camp and arrive breathless.

"I saw a lynx!" you shout to Joseph, the first person you see.

"How close was it?" he asks, his eyes wide.

"As close as you are to me," you say, realizing how close that really was, since Joseph is within arm's reach.

"Lynxes are usually awake at night," Joseph tells you. "It might have been roaming around in the early morning because it was hungry."

You feel the hair on your arms stand up. Good thing you scared it away.

After you hand Ma the firewood, she quickly fixes breakfast. Soon you are sinking your teeth into a stack of flapjacks and almost forget about the fact that maybe you could have been the morning meal of a big cat.

The wagon train starts rolling again a short while later. As you make your way higher into the Blue Mountains, the Trail has been getting harder to travel. Along the way, giant trees and branches lie in your path, making it difficult for the wagons to pass through. An hour after you start your day's hike today, another fallen tree blocks the way.

"Halt the wagons!" Caleb shouts. "We have to clear the path."

For the next two hours, the men of the wagon train work hard to chop up the tree and haul away the pieces. All the kids help by pulling large branches.

Everyone is exhausted by the time the work is done, but there's no time to rest. Caleb orders the wagons to start rolling again . . . until yet another tree needs to be cleared.

For the next several days, it's the same. The wagon train isn't covering much ground because you have to stop so frequently. Everyone is overtired, and tempers run short. It doesn't help that when the path is clear, the steep climbing is also slow and difficult. You, like everyone else, have blisters on the palms of your hands from dragging branches out of the way.

When Caleb finally halts the wagons for a midday rest, a man from the group starts to talk.

"We can keep moving at a snail's pace and

risk getting caught in more snow as we go up the mountains, or we can make a new plan," he says.

"Like what?" Pa asks.

"We could leave the wagons behind," he suggests. "We have only about two hundred and sixty miles to go before we're in Oregon City."

A few people snort and start to laugh. Leave the wagons behind! Ridiculous!

"Let's hear him out," Caleb says.

"If we just take what we need for the rest of the journey and tie it to the animals, we would move much more quickly," the man adds. "Plus, we have to think about how long our food supply will last if our trip lasts longer than expected."

Now some people murmur in agreement.

"Just think about it, everyone," Caleb says. "But for now, we have to keep moving."

You listen to Ma and Pa talk about what the man said.

"How could we possibly give up the wagon now?" Ma says. "We'd lose so much."

"Yes, but we do have to think about getting stuck

in the mountains in the colder weeks ahead if we keep moving so slowly," Pa says.

"But what if it gets better soon?" you ask.

"That's possible," Pa says, looking at each member of your family. "What do you think should we do?"

If you say you should abandon the wagon,
turn to page **28**

If you say you should keep the wagon,
turn to page **100**

You decide to see why Archie's so riled up and follow him. He continues to tug on your clothing and bark hysterically as he bounds away to the edge of camp. He leads you through the dark woods, whining, until finally, you smell something—it's not a skunk. It's smoke. Then, a glimmer of firelight just up ahead reveals that you and your wagon corral are not alone.

"*A campfire!*" you whisper, and grab Archie's collar, yanking him back. "Stay back, boy!" You

realize it's the smoke you saw through the trees earlier. But you don't know if these people are friendly.

Carefully, you edge closer to see who the strangers are. Against the firelight, you see several dark shapes, and you hear low voices. Your heart pounds as you overhear their conversation: they're gloating about all the unsuspecting wagon trains they've robbed on their final stretches to Oregon City. And, what's more, the bandits are talking about robbing *your* wagon train—tonight!

"Bandits, Archie!" you hiss. "Good job, boy!"

Together you slip away and rush back to camp, where you wake up Pa to warn him of the immediate danger.

"Good job," he tells you. "We could've lost everything." He hurries to wake Caleb, and they decide to tie up the bandits and bring them back with you to Oregon City so they can't continue to rob other unwitting travelers.

Pa orders you to stay with the wagons while they rush off to stop the bandits before they make their own sneak attack on your wagon train. Ma, Hannah, and Samuel are awake from all the commotion and are shocked at the events.

"I'm just glad you're safe," Ma says, hugging you tightly. "They could've seen you!"

Eliza and Joseph join your family near the campfire.

"I can't believe we were almost robbed in the middle of the night!" Joseph says.

"It was Archie," you tell him. "If I hadn't followed him, we never would have been warned in time."

Eliza leans down to scratch Archie's ears. "You saved us, boy!" she croons. "You're such a good dog. A hero!"

Archie licks her hand and barks in return.

Pa and Caleb return within the next couple of hours with three disgruntled bandits—all tied up together. It would be a funny sight if they still didn't look so menacing.

"What should we do with them?" Caleb asks.

"Tie them to the back of one of the wagons,"

says Pa. "They can walk with us the rest of the way to Oregon City. We'll deliver them to the local sheriff once we get there."

The bandits holler and grumble as they're forced to follow you the rest of the way.

"They're like the logs we used to drag behind the wagons earlier," Eliza whispers to you, giggling.

You can't help but grin and nod. Beside you, Archie bounds around your heels and growls at the bandits, ensuring they keep up.

Even though the journey the past several days has been especially exhausting, there's a new spring in your step as your wagon train rolls across the final miles of wooded country to Oregon City. Hannah and Samuel argue about who's going to eat what first. You can picture only a mouthwatering slice of chocolate cake.

When you finally step into Oregon City, you can hardly believe it. You've made it, after all. There are so many buildings—more than you even thought—and hundreds of people about. It's a real city, and a fresh start for your whole family.

Caleb and Pa find the local sheriff's station and deliver the bandits.

"We've been trying to track them down for months," the sheriff admits, wiping his forehead. "They've been robbing every poor traveler on the Oregon Trail. They know people are especially tired and vulnerable after the trek down from Laurel Hill, so that's when they strike."

"They almost got us, too," you add, "if it weren't for Archie! He showed us where they were hiding."

Archie tilts his head and sniffs the sheriff curiously. The sheriff's eyes widen.

"You don't say? Well, then, this little fella's a hero!" He digs into his pocket and fishes out a piece of jerky for Archie. "We can't thank you enough."

Eventually your family parts ways with the other wagon families. You're sad to say goodbye to Caleb, Joseph, and Eliza but know that you'll see them again.

Thanks to the little bit of money you still have left over, Pa is able to buy enough supplies to start your own farm on your newly claimed land. You help him build your very own cabin, and it's even bigger than your house back in Kentucky!

The first night in your cabin is the best you can ever remember. Ma piles steak, corn, and potatoes with fresh beans onto your plate. And as a special surprise, she makes a rich chocolate cake for dessert. You may even sneak another slice!

Everything has ended up just as you had hoped. It's been a long, hard few months on the Oregon Trail, but it's been worth the journey. Oregon City is everything you've imagined it would be and more. You've successfully completed your incredible journey West!

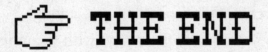 **THE END**

Oregon City

OCTOBER 6, 1850

GUIDE
to the Trail
THE FINAL STRETCH!

Congratulations on making it from Independence, Missouri, past Chimney Rock and through Devil's Gate all the way to Three Island Crossing, in what is now Idaho, on the Oregon Trail!

As you've already discovered in your travels across the prairie and desert terrain, surviving the journey of a lifetime requires you to be cautious and aware of your surroundings and to make smart decisions.

There's no substitute for being well prepared, so make sure to get all the information you need about what you will be facing ahead of time. This guide includes important facts about how to stay safe on the final leg of your trip across the Rocky Mountains to your destination, Oregon City! Read up, and get rolling on the Trail!

DANGERS!

CROSSING RIVERS

Crossing rivers can be necessary but always presents great risk. If you are unfamiliar with the river, you can quickly lose control of your raft to river rapids, which will dash your raft against the rocks. If you fall in, hypothermia likely isn't too far behind—the water is sure to be very cold. If you can, try to find someone more familiar with the river's navigation to help you across.

SAFETY IN NUMBERS

While it may be tempting to split up for various reasons, sticking together is better than going off alone in almost every situation. People in pioneer days didn't have ways to quickly communicate long-distance with one another, and if something happens to one part of the split-up group, the other won't have any way of knowing until it's too late.

RUGGED TERRAIN

Trekking through the mountains is treacherous and slow going. Look for roads and paths people have built before you, and be wary of cliffs and inclines, where it may be too steep to lower your wagons with ropes. You may need to weigh down the wagons to slow their descent.

FIRE

Stamp out campfires completely after use. If you become cold throughout the night, try to find extra blankets and layers, as it is dangerous to fall asleep in front of a campfire. You could catch fire before you even wake up.

DISEASE

Cholera and dysentery are common on the Trail. Many travelers died from contaminated food and water, so be sure your food is cooked and clean, and your water fully boiled. Rabies is also a danger in wild animals, and they can pass it on to your animals, who can pass it on to you. Do not touch wild animals or your own if they've been bitten. In the colder temperatures, frostbite and gangrene can be common if you don't have enough layers, which can result in loss of limbs and even death. Be sure to have thick, sturdy walking shoes so you don't lose your toes!

WEATHER

Be prepared to travel through a vast range of weather systems, ranging from bone-chilling snowstorms to bristling hot desert days. Even in the warmer months, sudden snowstorms still occur in higher rocky areas. Be sure to stick together and keep as many supplies as you can. Avalanches can also occur in higher elevations where there are fewer trees, so stay where the foliage is thick. If you fall into an icy lake and are trapped under the ice, be sure to look for spots that are lighter—this means there is no snow covering the ice, and it may be the hole through which you fell. In hotter, desert-like conditions, be wary of extreme fatigue, your wagon getting stuck in sand dunes, and lack of water leading to dehydration and death for you and your animals. If possible, avoid areas like this altogether, as you likely won't get far.

WILDLIFE

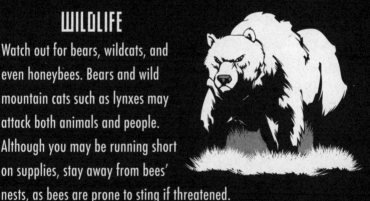

Watch out for bears, wildcats, and even honeybees. Bears and wild mountain cats such as lynxes may attack both animals and people. Although you may be running short on supplies, stay away from bees' nests, as bees are prone to sting if threatened.

DISHONEST PEOPLE

Sometimes people take advantage of others on the Trail, so be wary of passing traders. Bandits are infamous for attacking unsuspecting wagon trains at night. Stay on your guard.

THE Journey FROM Three Island Crossing TO Oregon City

Oregon City

THE DALLES

FLAGSTAFF HILL

OREGON TERRITORY

Three Island Crossing

FORT BOISE

CALIFORNIA

UTAH TERRITORY

Legend

Oregon Trail ◄━◼━◼━◼
TERRITORIES ━━━━━
State Lines ━━━━━
(Modern Day)

👉 FINDING YOUR WAY

In 1850, there aren't roads or many signs, and the maps are not very precise, particularly as you make your way into the mountains. There aren't even states yet. You have to navigate by using a compass and by keeping a sharp eye out for famous landmarks. The Trail is difficult to follow, particularly as you make your way into the mountains. Never leave the Trail or your group, and don't take shortcuts. Weather can be unpredictable in the mountains—keep a sharp eye at all times if you want to reach Oregon!

Look for these landmarks between and near Three Island Crossing and Oregon City

DISTANCE FROM INDEPENDENCE, MISSOURI:

FORT BOISE: 1,426 miles (2,295 km)

FLAGSTAFF HILL: 1,535 miles (2,470 km)

THE DALLES: 1,732 miles (2,787 km)

The Oregon Trail™

LIVE the Adventure!

Do you have what it takes to make it all the way to Oregon City?

Look straight into the face of danger and dysentery.

Read all four books in this new choose-your-own-trail series!